*To Paul, who helps me see the
possibilities instead of the obstacles.*

✳

CONTENTS

A needle-made lace constructed totally of thread on skeleton base threads and formed into small squares called motifs. The motifs are beautiful framed and they make wonderful wedding gifts. They can also be formed into patterns on accent pillows or used as special quilt pieces.

Open designs worked on firmly woven linen, mostly in buttonhole stitches with portions cut away to achieve a lacy, "open window" effect. It has traditionally been used on table linens, quilt blocks, pillows, and such decorative items as bellpulls, but it creates a striking effect when used on collars, cuffs, the front pieces of a blouse, and aprons.

Norwegian immigrants brought this beautiful embroidery to America. It is worked in kloster blocks to form geometric designs with woven bars, filling stitches, and cut-away portions. It is used for the most exquisite table linens, but small, quick touches of Hardanger are wonderful as border designs for clothing, curtains, and such small gifts as key holders.

A needlework crafter's delight! A sturdy needlework lace brought to America by Danish settlers, traditionally used to trim the edges of table runners, placemats, and napkin corners, but also striking as an insert on collars and cuffs, quilts, and even baby clothes. Try it on window dressings for a special "mood" effect.

The author at work.

ACKNOWLEDGMENTS

Most of my thanks must go to my husband, Paul, and my children, who not only supported me through the year-long process of writing this book, but through a pregnancy at the same time. Each of them is very special to me.

Thanks to my mother, Janice Holmgren, for the many hours spent setting up the photographs and her patience in doing them more than once while I learned to operate my new camera.

Thanks to the women who shared their talents, patterns, and treasured articles with me: Agnes Bishop, Lota Brinton, Helen Hansen, and Mary Ann Holman.

Thanks to A. J. Simmonds, head of the historical archives at Utah State University, for his help in research.

Thanks to Eric Rasmussen for sharing his photography skills.

Thanks to the cute little girls who were so cooperative about posing for photographs: Alissa Harman, Jamie Harman, Tanna Hollingsworth, Nicodee Holmes, Katherine Hutchison, Skye Longhurst, Kristi Strong, and Shellie Strong.

Thanks to all those who contributed items to be photographed: Candace Daly, Suzanne Ferry, Mary Gardner, Clixie Hollingsworth, Margo Holmes, Melanie Holmgren, Phyllis Holmgren, LaRue Kingston, Beryl Nelson, and Suzanne Strong.

And last, but hardly least, thanks to my editor, Adrienne Ingrum, who patiently guided me through this exciting new experience!

Four generations at work.

INTRODUCTION

At almost every wedding reception in Box Elder County (northern Utah), you can be sure a beautiful trousseau will be displayed including pieced quilts, tatted doilies, handkerchiefs decorated with netting, and any item you could possibly use to stock a linen closet, all trimmed with embroidery or handmade lace.

By my late teen years, not only did I have a cedar chest bulging with heirloom pieces, I had learned from my mother and grandmothers the methods used to produce many of them. The patterns have been collected over five generations, and in some instances the original articles have been preserved. In interviewing women for this book, I have been shown precious crafted items that have come down through ten generations.

Only after moving away from the area for several years did I realize how rare my treasures actually are. I found that I had neighbors who thought all lace was machine-made. They made quick converts, however, when they realized that they, too, could learn the seemingly impossible methods of making lace by hand.

The love of needlework has traditionally been passed from mother to daughter not only by handing down treasured handcrafted articles, but by spending wonderful hours together learning the needlework techniques. But unlike our mothers and grandmothers, most of us cannot take for granted

*Cedar chest overflowing with
trousseau treasures typically seen at
northern Utah wedding receptions.*

*Agnes Bishop instructs her
granddaughter, Clixie Hollingsworth,
in the vanishing art of netting,
explained in chapter 5.*

The author working on one of her many in-progress projects.

having a range of needlework techniques that we can easily learn from family members or neighbors. Even in rural communities many needle arts are disappearing as the older generations pass away, and even where you can find a young person who has been wise enough to learn the old techniques, many of the basic, everyday designs and patterns have not been maintained. I leave to historians, folklorists, and museum curators the preservation of the intricate, one-of-a-kind needlecrafted items. My concern is to show the beginner how easy, exciting, and rewarding it is to *do* these needle arts and how patterns that are generations old can be used to trim the most chic outfits and decorate the smartest furnishings of our computer age.

Today, in spite of our hi-tech society and the availability of well-made, mass-produced clothing and furnishings, women (and men, too) crave that singular, special item that was hand-made with love and care, and they are rediscovering the joy of doing fine needlework.

You can easily learn these techniques by following the instructions in this book. I hope to spread not only the techniques and the patterns but some of the joy of doing these needlework projects. At any given time while I was growing up there would be several projects in progress in my home and the homes of women I knew, but they were not "pressure projects." The women I learned from relax with their needlework, picking it up whenever they sit down. Not having to think about what their hands are doing in many cases, they create masterpieces in thread. I know many women who keep their needlework baskets right next to their purses and never go anywhere without taking both along. These women make lace in hospital waiting rooms, at Little League ballgame halftimes, riding back and forth to town, and even on airplanes. You would be surprised how many people express an interest in the articles being made and show wonder at the techniques involved. That is the only bad side effect to a needlework addiction: once you become proficient at it, everyone admires your work and you end up giving a lot of it away, for it makes unique gifts.

This, then, is the reason for this book, not to give a full history or a complete guide to each of the methods discussed, but rather to provide basic guidelines for the beginner to my favorite vanishing American needle arts. Like most things American, these needle arts are not indigenous, but were transplanted and improvised upon by the people from many nations who came to America. And also like most things American, these needle arts were adapted to changes in materials, uses (a keystone of American needle arts was that something beautiful still had to be useful), and pattern style until each needle arts technique, no matter what its roots, has become an American genre.

With a bit of patience, I am sure you will be delighted with your handiwork, and before long will be creating the pieces that your children and grand-children will treasure in years to come.

A glossary at the end of the book will help everyone to know what is meant by the needlework terms used. A list of sources for the necessary supplies is also included, with mail order addresses which will make these supplies available to those in even the most remote areas of the country.

Key to Pronunciation Symbols*

a	fat
ā	ape
ä	car
e	ten
ē	even
i	is
ō	go
ūr	urn

Aemilia-ars—(ə mē′ lēə - ärs)
Cutwork—(kut′ wūrk)
Hardanger—(här′ dāng r)
Hedebo—(hed ē′ bō)
Netting—(net′ in)
Smocking—(smäk′ in)
Tatting—(tat′ in)
Teneriffe—(ten′ ə ref)

*From *Webster's New World Dictionary*, 1977, William Collins & World Publishing Co., Inc.

Cedar chest.

Pillow with an Aemilia-ars lace motif.

Colored Cutwork tablecloth.

Hardanger dresser scarf for a dining buffet.

Hardanger tablecloth.

ERIC L. RASMUSSEN

Hedebo insert on a book cover.

Hedebo edged towel.

VANISHING
AMERICAN
NEEDLE
ARTS

Netted doilies.

1

AEMILIA-ARS LACE

This needle-made lace is worked in squares called motifs and reminds me of a stained glass window because of the geometric designs. It is one of the rarer forms of lace today, and besides the items which I have made in recent years, I have only seen one other project decorated with Aemilia-ars lace. The pillowcases my Grandmother Hansen used in her guest room many years ago had a border made of this kind of lace. There is no way to tell exactly how old they were, but I am sure they were part of her trousseau. She probably made them herself before her marriage on September 10, 1919. My interest was sparked by those pillowcases, and the motif photographed in figure 1 is very similar to the ones she used.

An Aemilia-ars lace motif is constructed entirely of thread on its own lattice base or skeleton, and after completion is inserted into a piece of fabric.

I was not able to find any information about the origins and variations of Aemilia-ars lace, but in the course of researching, I did discover that at the end of the nineteenth century a society was organized to preserve this art. I would love to hear more about this society if it still exists, but so far I have been unable to find any information concerning it.

Because so little printed material is available on Aemilia-ars lace, the patterns described here are all originals. The motifs can be joined side to side, in a triangular shape, or can be inserted singly. Table linens would look

Off-white Aemilia-ars lace motif set into an antique satin pillow and backed with a rust colored fabric.

3

beautiful with a motif inserted at each corner, and a framed motif makes a striking wall hanging.

Supplies Needed

* A piece of thin cardboard approximately 8 inches square, covered on one side with a plain colored fabric.
* DMC Pearl Cotton size 5
* Any extra-strong thread in a contrasting color (J & P Coats Dual Duty Plus Extra Strong Button and Carpet Thread works very well)

* Regular sewing needle
* Darning needle
* Sharp scissors
* Number 2 pencil
* Rubber cement

Construction

Secure the plain fabric to the cardboard with rubber cement. Then, with the fabric side up, draw the pattern shown in figure 2 directly onto the fabric-covered cardboard making sure that the lines meet exactly at the corners.

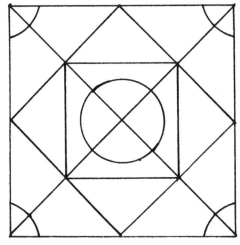

Figure 2

Aemilia-ars lace motif pattern to be transferred onto the fabric-backed cardboard.

Bar tacks hold the skeleton to the cardboard and keep it tight until the entire motif is completed; make pinholes at each of the intersections to mark where they should be placed. To make the bar tacks use a regular sewing needle and the extra strong button and carpet thread. Follow figure 3, coming up through 1 and down through 2, then up through 3 and down through 4, and so on—just like the old sewing cards you played with as a child.

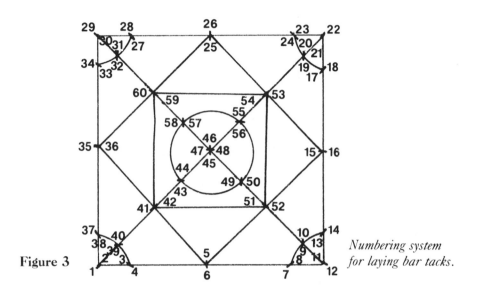

Figure 3

Numbering system for laying bar tacks.

Thread the darning needle with a long length of the DMC Pearl Cotton. Start at the lower right corner. Do not knot your thread. (To keep the thread tight, you may find it easier to wind this starting thread around a pin and secure it to the fabric-covered cardboard along the edge—away from the design.) Build the skeleton by passing the thread under each of the bar tacks along the outside edge of the square until you reach the starting point the second time. This will leave you back at the lower right corner, with a double thread all the way around the outside of the motif. These threads need to be pulled tight.

Next, work the diagonal: go under the center bar tacks, through the upper left corner bar tack (make sure you go under and over the threads of the skeleton at the corner). Now go back through the lower right corner the same way, and back through the upper left corner a second time, always remembering to go under the center bar tacks. This will make the diagonal three threads thick.

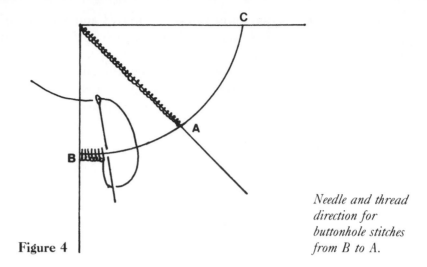

Figure 4

Needle and thread direction for buttonhole stitches from B to A.

Now cord the diagonal skeleton threads (see figure 4) back to point A by winding the needle thread around and around the three base threads. When you reach point A, slip the thread under the bar tack; extend your thread to point B, and go over and through the bar tack and around the skeleton threads at B. To make the base thread three thick, go through A once again and back through B a second time. Cover the base threads from B to A with a buttonhole stitch as shown in figure 4.

The needle should go *under* the base threads and point toward the center of the motif, but then back over the needle thread before it is tightened. These stitches should be close and even, but not extremely tight.

After reaching point A with the buttonhole stitches, slip under the bar tack again and lay three base threads between A and C using the same procedure you followed on the B-to-A side. Use buttonhole stitches to cover the base threads from C back to A by throwing your thread in the opposite direction. See figure 5. If you find it easier, you can turn the piece to work the C-to-A side as long as you follow the needle and thread directions in figure 5.

Now you have reached point A again. Slip the thread under the bar tack once more; finish cording clear into the center of the design and slip the thread under the crossed bar tacks. From here, you are going to lay the three base threads to the bottom left corner, ending there and cording back to what would be point A in the lower left corner. Finish the B-to-A and C-to-A legs with buttonhole stitches as explained above and then cord to the center bar

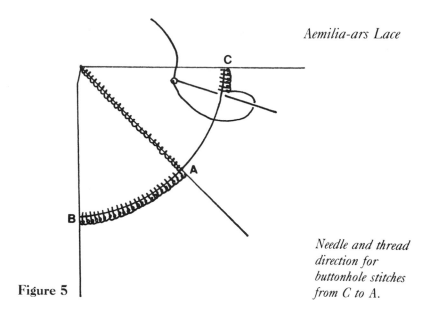

C

A

B

Figure 5

*Needle and thread
direction for
buttonhole stitches
from C to A.*

tacks again. At this point the two diagonals on the left side have been completed. Slip the thread under the center cross bars to lay the three base threads to the upper right corner as shown in figure 6.

Cord, stitch, and cord this diagonal back to the center just like the other two.

The remainder of the motif will be finished from the center point out. After slipping under the center bar tacks for the last time, cord down the

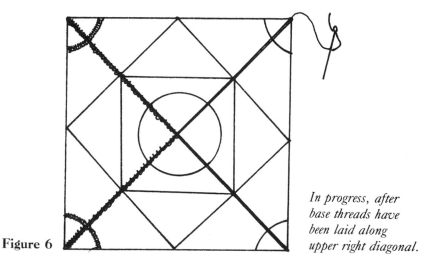

Figure 6

*In progress, after
base threads have
been laid along
upper right diagonal.*

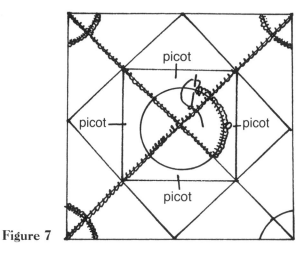

Figure 7

Picot placements. Needle and thread direction for circle buttonhole stitches.

lower right diagonal until you reach the point where the circle crosses it. Slip under the bar tack and then continue around the circle, going under each bar tack and wrapping the thread around each diagonal bar as you cross it, until you have made one circle with the base thread. This single base thread will be covered with buttonhole stitches. Figure 7 demonstrates the thread and needle positions.

When you have stitched halfway around the first quarter of the circle (you are on the extreme right side), you will leave a small loop of thread called a picot between the buttonhole stitches. To make the picot, illustrated in figure 7, just don't pull the thread tight on one stitch, and then hold the loop with a finger while you complete the following stitch. This is shown in figure 8. Continue around the circle with buttonhole stitches, making a picot at the center point between each diagonal.

After you have completed the circle, slip under the bar tack and continue cording down the diagonal base threads toward the lower right corner. When you reach the point where both squares cross the diagonal, slip under the bar tack and lay a single base thread around the small square. Then lay a base thread around the large square by passing the thread under the bar tacks, wrapping the needle thread once around each of the existing skeleton bar threads as you cross them. Follow the thread direction shown in figure 9.

Working from E in the direction shown in figure 9, form buttonhole stitches along each side of the center square all the way around, forming the motif to the point shown in figure 10.

To make the first triangle, use a buttonhole stitch and work from E to F

8

Figure 8

Picots in progress.

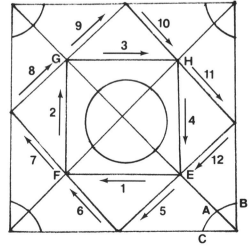

Figure 9

Thread direction for laying the inside and outside squares.

Figure 10

Buttonhole stitches completed on inside square.

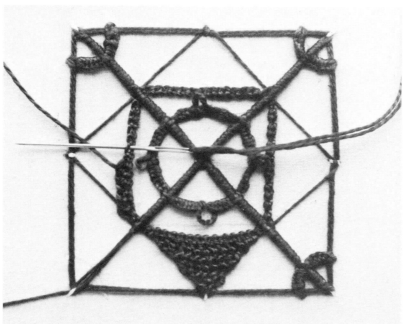

Figure 11

Building the triangles in solid buttonhole stitches.

(see figure 9). The second row is connected to the first row by pushing the needle down through the tops of the stitches that are already there. To make the triangle shape, place the stitches of the new row in between the stitches of the previous row, making fewer stitches in each row. Figure 11 illustrates this procedure.

Be sure to catch the side threads at the end and the beginning of each row. (Each triangle will have the same number of rows and end in a point when completed.) At the point, catch the skeleton base threads at the outer edge of the motif and then work the thread in and out of the edge of the triangle to come back to point F.

Working from F to G (see figure 9), complete the left triangle the same way; then the top triangle and, finally, the right triangle. This brings you back to the lower right diagonal.

Finish cording toward the lower right corner to A (where the little legs stick out). Slip under the bar tack, lay the three base threads, and buttonhole stitch back as you did on the other diagonals. Unpin the starting thread and lay it back along this diagonal. Cover it along with the base threads as you cord back to the corner. Cut off any of the starting thread that might extend beyond the cording.

To finish the motif, run an overcasting stitch around the outside skeleton base threads and make a small knot at the bottom right corner. See figure 12.

To detach the motif, cut the bar tack threads from the back of the cardboard.

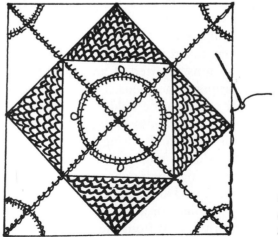

Figure 12

Overcasting the outside skeleton threads.

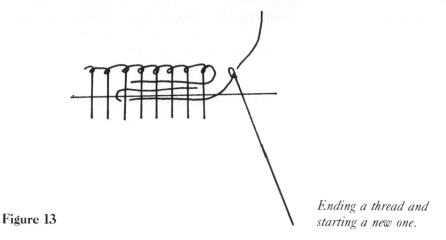

Figure 13

Ending a thread and starting a new one.

NOTE: When you find it necessary to rethread your needle with pearl cotton use the following procedure. Secure the old thread by running it back under a few of the last stitches made, then cut it off. Rethread the needle with a new length of thread and again run it under a few of the previous stitches in the same direction as the old thread. Then, coming over *one* stitch, thread it back under the same stitches in the other direction and continue covering the skeleton threads as shown in figure 13.

Finishing Techniques

To block your Aemilia-ars lace motif, remove it from the cardboard backing and place it face down on a thick towel on an ironing board. Secure the motif at the corners, using pins inserted at an angle. Be sure to keep the motif square and at the proper dimensions. Use pins to secure any other areas of the design that might need to be held. See figure 14.

At this point your motif should look exactly like the patterned drawing that you started with in figure 2. Using spray starch, spray the motif *lightly*, then cover the entire design with a damp press cloth. With your iron on a medium hot (cotton) setting, set it right over the motif and press down slightly until the press cloth is dry. Do not slide the iron back and forth at all. Allow the motif to sit undisturbed for a couple of hours until you are certain it is completely dry. Then unpin it from the towel.

Figure 14   *Blocking the finished motif.*

To prepare the piece of cloth into which you are going to insert the motif, cut the cloth to whatever size is needed for your finished project. If you are making a pillow, cut the cloth ⅝ of an inch bigger all around than you want the finished size of the pillow to be. (For example, if you want the finished pillow to be 12 inches square, cut a 13¼-inch square of fabric. This allows for the outer seam allowances in the pillow construction.) If you are framing the piece, it is best to allow an extra 1½ inches all the way around. (If your frame is 5 × 7, your fabric should measure 6½ × 8½.) This way you will have enough fabric to secure firmly to the back of a 5-by-7-inch piece of illustration board, which will later be fastened into the frame. Press this piece of cloth out flat and mark the center point with a pin.

Mark a 2⅜-inch square around the center point (this is what one side of your motif should measure). Then mark another square, ¼-inch smaller as shown in figure 15, inside the first. (If, on some projects, you want to insert the motifs along the edge or in some other design, you will have to adjust the placement of the openings accordingly.)

Cut along the dotted lines of the inner square and make small slashes to the corners of the outer square. Fold along the solid lines and press the flaps to the wrong side.

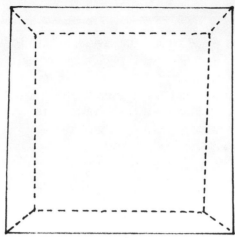

Figure 15

Pattern for fabric into which the motif will be set. Cut along dotted lines and fold flaps back.

Figure 16   *Buttonhole stitch used to attach motif to fabric.*

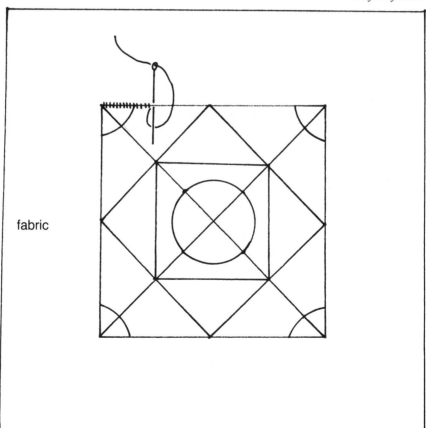

fabric

Place the motif into the opening and secure it on the back with masking tape placed diagonally over the corners. (The motif should fit exactly flush with the edges of the opening.)

Lay the entire piece out flat and right side up on a table top and attach the outside skeleton of the motif to the fabric using buttonhole stitches as shown in figure 16, removing the tape as necessary.

Now take another piece of fabric exactly the same size as the first and place it so the right side will show behind the motif. Sew the two pieces of fabric together along the outside edge.

Suggested Uses

* Framed as in the figure below (this makes a lovely wedding gift)

* Small accent pillow as in figure 17

* Quilts

* Joined side by side and inserted into a pillowcase as in figure 18

To join motifs, lay them face to face, two at a time, on a flat surface after

Framed Aemilia-ars lace motifs.

15

Figure 17

Close-up details of an Aemilia-ars lace motif set into accent pillow.

Figure 18

Three motifs joined side to side and inserted into a pillowcase. An especially effective treatment when colored thread is used to construct the lace and the motifs are set into a white or ecru pillowcase. A piece of fabric can be placed behind the set-in lace as a liner for added accent.

Figure 19

Three motifs set together in a triangular shape and inserted in the corner of a tablecloth. To achieve the most striking result, use a dark colored thread to construct the lace.

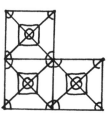

they have been blocked, and stitch the outside skeleton threads together with an overcast stitch as shown in figure 12.

* Joined in a triangular shape and inserted into the corners of a tablecloth as shown in figure 19

Additional Patterns

Instructions for Figure 20

The motif shown in figure 20 is the one that I used on the accent pillow (see figure 17). To construct this motif, use the same basic procedure described for the previous one. Make the bar tacks, lay the outside skeleton threads, then the first diagonal. Cord to point A, then work the legs with buttonhole stitches leaving a picot at the center as shown in figure 20. After cording to the center of the third diagonal, start cording the upper right diagonal working from the center out. When you reach point B, lay two base threads for the center square and then buttonhole stitch over them. Continue cording up the diagonal to point C, lay a single base thread for the larger square and then the octagon shape working each time in a counter-clockwise direction. Buttonhole stitch over the base thread of the square and then work the triangle shapes as you did on the first motif (see figure 1) described in this chapter. Complete the motif by finishing the fourth corner.

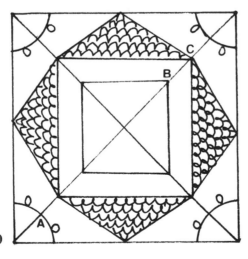

Figure 20

Pattern for the finished motif shown in figure 17.

Figure 21

Figure 22

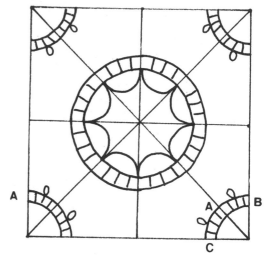

Pattern for the three motifs shown in figure 18.

Pattern with doubled circles. Rungs between the circles are not difficult to construct, yet give the design an intricate look. It should be used for a project such as a framed grouping that won't take a lot of wear and tear since it is very loosely constructed.

Figure 23

Figure 24

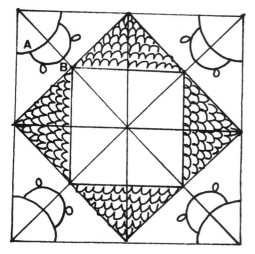

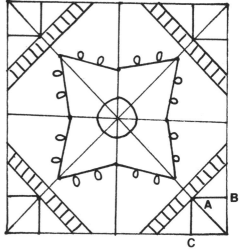

Pattern with picots in the corners. This would look nice set into a solid-colored accent pillow quilted in the same color thread as the lace.

Pattern with a very open, loose design would be very effective worked in a pastel color and backed with a darker shade of the same hue.

Instructions for Figure 21

The motif in figure 21 is lovely set into a pillowcase as shown in figure 18. Instead of cording the diagonals it is worked with a buttonhole stitch throughout. The cross-bar skeleton threads are worked after the third diagonal and corner are completed by taking the needle under the bar tack at A, then buttonhole stitching back to the center. Go under the bar tack at B, then buttonhole stitch back to the center again. Work C and D in the same way. As on the previous motifs, the inside designs are worked from the center out as you complete the fourth diagonal.

Instructions for Figure 22

The only difference between working the motif shown in figure 22 and the previous ones is the little rungs between the two legs on each diagonal. See A on figure 22. To do this, make both legs as shown. Then when the motif is completed go back with a new thread. Slip through the top ridge of the buttonhole stitches on the outer leg at A (this will secure your thread), to the first rung. Pass the thread over to the inner leg and through the buttonhole stitches there in the same way to the next rung. Continue back and forth between the legs like this on each diagonal using a separate thread in each corner.

The double circle rungs in the inside of the motif are worked the same way.

To work the cross bar skeleton threads, see the directions for figure 21.

Instructions for Figure 23

The motif in figure 23 has different legs in the corners. To work them, lay the three base threads from the diagonal as before, and buttonhole stitch back to point A. At this point lay three base threads between A and B. Buttonhole stitch from B to the picot, leave the little loop, and buttonhole stitch back to A. From here buttonhole stitch to the diagonal and complete the other leg.

To work the cross bar skeleton threads, see the directions for figure 21.

Instructions for Figure 24

For the motif shown in figure 24, make three legs in each corner. The method of completing the rungs between the second and third legs is described in the directions for figure 22.

To work the cross bar skeleton threads, see the directions for figure 21.

2

CUTWORK

I particularly love this form of needlework because of its elaborate detail. The beautiful open designs are worked on firmly woven fabric and the finished work looks like an old-fashioned valentine. Cutwork was brought to America from Italy, where it evolved from Venetian needlepoint lace. There are many different types of cutwork, including, in order of difficulty and intricacy, simple, Renaissance, Richelieu, and Italian. All these types of cutwork look similar, yet each has unique characteristics which classify it into its own group.

The design is traced on the fabric and then outlined with very close buttonhole, satin, and outline stitches. Portions of the fabric are then cut away to create an airy effect. In places where the section of fabric to be cut away is large, little bars or "brides" are used to reinforce the work. Cutwork can be very time-consuming if the pattern is very elaborate, and that is one reason this type of needlework is not done a lot today.

Simple cutwork is displayed so that each petal, leaf, or stem of a flower touches another, making the design secure in itself when the in-between spaces are cut away. See figure 26.

In Renaissance cutwork the little bars or brides are added to secure the design, which seems to float inside the cut-away space. There are quite a few different methods of working these bars. They range from woven to

This cutwork tablecloth, once my grandmother Thorsen's, and now my mother's, is just big enough to fit a tea table.

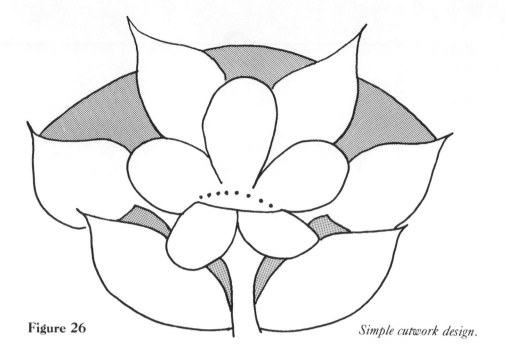

Figure 26

Simple cutwork design.

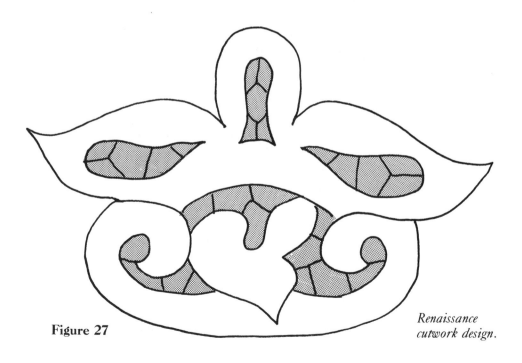

Figure 27

*Renaissance
cutwork design.*

buttonholed and from a simple bar attaching two points to a five-legged filling with a separate ring attached to the center. The bars are the emphasized characteristic of this form of cutwork and should be used extensively to create an airy, lacelike effect. See figure 27.

The only thing that distinguishes Richelieu cutwork from Renaissance are the tiny picots that are worked onto the bars, and for this reason the two types are often mistaken for each other. When working picots you can use either the loop, bullion, or buttonhole methods which are explained later in this chapter. Because these picots are the only difference between the two types of cutwork, the same designs may be used when constructing either. See figure 28 for a pattern for Richelieu cutwork.

Italian cutwork is done in small squares in which some of the fabric threads have been removed and others left to work the stitches into. The border of

Figure 28   *Richelieu cutwork design.*

Figure 29

*Italian
cutwork
design.*

the square and the threads that are left are woven, and then intricate filling stitches are used to fill in the spaces. A lot of surface embroidery is done in between the squares, too. See figure 29.

Years ago most cutwork designs were worked in floral patterns, but recently I have seen a few articles done with modern geometric lines. This technique is used primarily for table linens, but adapts itself very well for accent pillows, wall hangings, and stylish clothing.

Supplies Needed

* Embroidery hoops (if you don't have a good 8- or 10-inch pair of wooden ones with a screw tightener, it would be best to invest in a pair before you begin your cutwork project)
* A 12-inch-square piece of firmly woven, medium weight fabric, such as kettlecloth

* Transfer pencil and tissue paper
* Sharp darning needle size 20
* DMC Pearl Cotton size 5
* Sharp scissors

Figure 30

Cutwork design worked on a solid-colored fabric, then attached to an apron pocket.

Figure 31

Close-up details of pocket design shown above.

Construction

Trace the pattern in figure 32 on a piece of tissue paper. Next, so that the design won't be stamped on your fabric backward, flip the tissue paper over and trace the same lines on the other side with the transfer pencil. Press hard so the lines are dark, but blow away any specks of the transfer pencil that are left so they will not mark the fabric.

Using a medium hot iron, with the transfer pencil side of the tissue paper down, press the design onto the fabric, being careful not to slide the paper.

Place the fabric securely in the embroidery hoops. Thread your needle and bring it up at point A. See figure 33. Leave the thread end, about $1/_8$ of an inch, loose (it will be covered later with buttonhole stitches). Make a running stitch around the entire outside edge of the design working in a counter-clockwise direction. When you have reached point A again, make a second row of running stitches being careful not to pull any of them too tight. When you reach point A after the second round, switch to a buttonhole stitch, as shown in figure 33, and continue around one more time.

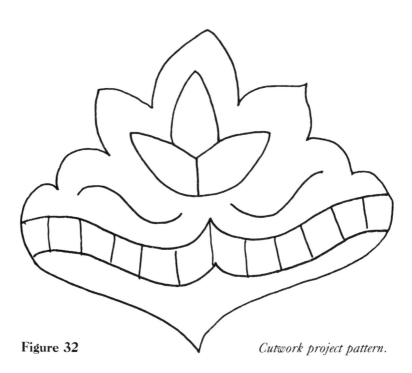

Figure 32   *Cutwork project pattern.*

Figure 33

*Running stitches and
buttonhole stitches.*

When your thread starts to become too short to work with, don't knot it. Instead, make a few running stitches along the design outline where the next buttonhole stitches will cover them, and cut the end of the thread. This will leave the work smooth and you won't run the risk of cutting a knot off when trimming the cutaway portions. To start with a new thread, take two or three running stitches in the opposite direction you are working; then bring the needle up from the back through the last buttonhole stitch that was worked. See figure 34.

When doing cutwork, always remember that the edge of the buttonhole stitch that has the little ridge must be toward the sections that are to be cut away. (In the event that both sides of a line are to be cut, it is necessary to use overlapping buttonhole stitches as shown in figure 35, working first in

Figure 34

new thread
old thread

*Starting with
new thread.*

Figure 35

*Double-sided
buttonhole stitch.*

Figure 36

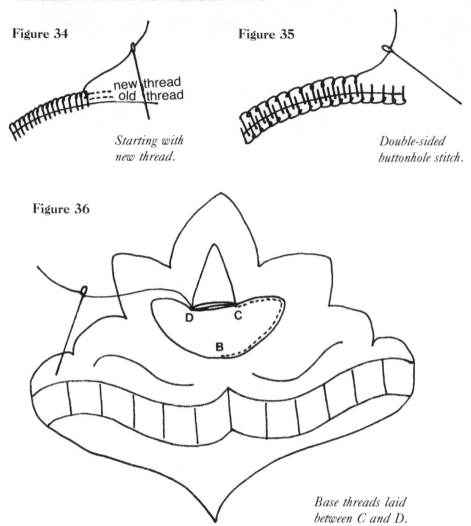

D C

B

*Base threads laid
between C and D.*

one direction and then the other. This method will not be used on any of the designs you are working in this chapter, but is illustrated for future reference, when you may want to work your own designs.)

After completing the buttonhole stitches back to point A (see figure 33), secure the thread by taking it through to the back and running it over and under a few of the stitches and then cutting it off.

Bring the needle up again at point B (see figure 36) and make running stitches to point C. Take the needle across the top of the fabric to point D, and take a tiny stitch to catch the thread into the fabric right *on* the pattern line. Then come back across to point C and take another tiny stitch. Now, lay the third thread across by going back to point D and taking a second stitch. These stitches should be just loose enough to allow you to pull them down into the Y in the next step without causing the pattern to lose its shape or the fabric to pucker.

Being careful only to catch the three threads and not the fabric behind them, cover half the space between D and C with buttonhole stitches, bringing the needle up from the bottom. This will put the ridge on the top side. When you reach the center point, take the needle behind the three threads (again, do not catch the fabric), and take a tiny stitch at point B. Take the needle back over and around the three threads at the point where the buttonhole stitches ended, and come back down to B and take another tiny stitch. This will lay the three base threads and, if pulled tight, should pull the C/D line down to form a Y as shown in figure 37.

Buttonhole-stitch over the three lower threads back to the intersection and then continue buttonhole stitching the right arm of the Y to point C. From here, continue the first row of running stitches, working counter-clockwise from point C to D to B; then come completely around again to leave a second row of running stitches. The top inset design at this point consists of two rows of running stitches around the outside edge, and a Y made of buttonhole stitches that is attached to the fabric only at points B, C, and D. See figure 38.

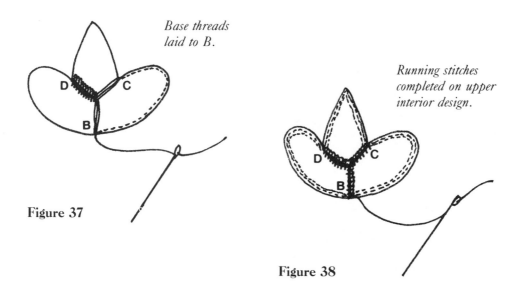

Base threads
laid to B.

Figure 37

Running stitches
completed on upper
interior design.

Figure 38

Outline this inset with buttonhole stitches. Work with the needle moving toward the center so the ridge will be on the inside, just as you did on the larger design. Secure the thread from the back by running it over and under a few buttonhole stitches as you did before, and cut it off.

Bring the needle up about a quarter of an inch toward the middle from point E (figure 39), and take a few little running stitches back to point E. This will secure the thread in starting.

Using a stem stitch as shown in figure 40, work to point F; then take your needle across the back of the fabric and come up at point G. Stem stitch from G to H and make a tiny knot to tie off the thread from the back side of the fabric.

To complete the part of the design that resembles a ladder, bring the

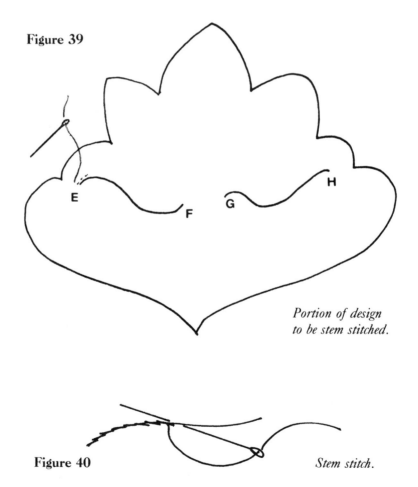

Figure 39

E F G H

*Portion of design
to be stem stitched.*

Figure 40 *Stem stitch.*

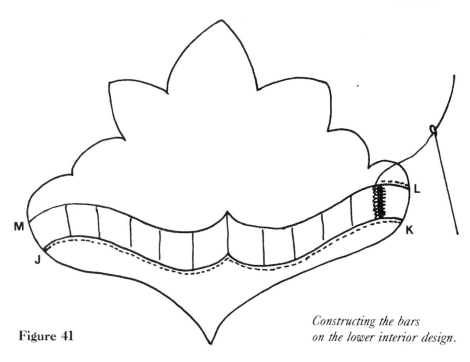

Figure 41

Constructing the bars on the lower interior design.

needle up at point J (see figure 41) and make running stitches all the way across to point K. Slip the needle under the buttonhole stitches from the back to point L, and make running stitches to the first rung of the ladder. Lay three base threads. This will leave you at the bottom. Then buttonhole stitch over them until you reach the top side of the ladder again. (Be careful once again not to catch the fabric here as it will be cut away later.)

Continue with the running stitches between the rungs. At each rung, lay the three base threads, and buttonhole stitch back to the top until you reach point M. Slip the needle under the buttonhole stitches on the back again between M and J. Now, working toward point K, make buttonhole stitches over the running stitches, catching the fabric and the edge of each rung. Bring the needle from the bottom up, leaving the ridge of the stitches on the top side. At point K, once again run the needle under the stitches on the back coming up at L. The buttonhole stitches on this side of the ladder will be made by bringing the needle down from the top (see figure 42), so the ridge will be on the bottom side. (With the ridges facing each other, you will be able to cut the fabric between them away.)

When you have reached point M and secured your thread all the stitching

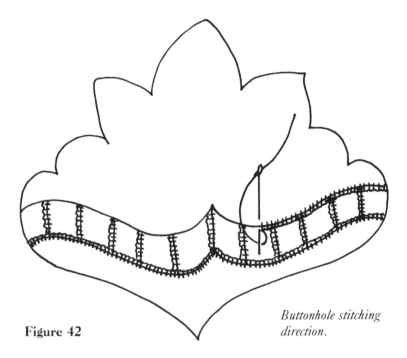

Figure 42

Buttonhole stitching direction.

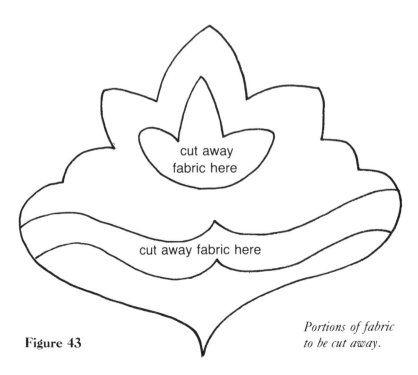

cut away
fabric here

cut away fabric here

Figure 43

Portions of fabric to be cut away.

Figure 44

Figure 45

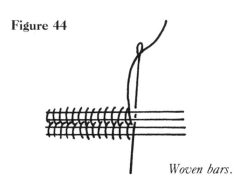

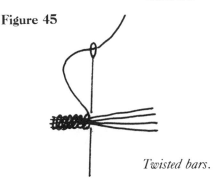

Woven bars.

Twisted bars.

on the design is completed. You can now trim the fabric away behind the brides. See figure 43. Be careful when trimming to get as close to the stitching as possible so there won't be a ragged edge left. This requires a very sharp pair of scissors. Do not at any point cut any of the stitches, only the fabric.

When working the bars, or brides, in place of the buttonhole stitch used on the previous project, you may use a woven bar (see figure 44) or a twisted bar (see figure 45). Of these, the buttonholed bar is used most often because it is sturdiest.

Picots for Richelieu Projects

When working the picots for the Richelieu projects, you may use any of the following three methods.

The *loop* method, which is the easiest, is worked around a pin that is inserted right into the fabric. (See figure 46.) The working thread is placed under the pinhead, then up over the base threads of the bar and behind them. The needle is then inserted behind the loop on the pin and through the loop formed by the working thread before it is pulled tight. The finished picot is shown in figure 47.

Figure 46

Figure 47

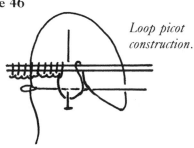

Loop picot construction.

Completed loop picot.

33

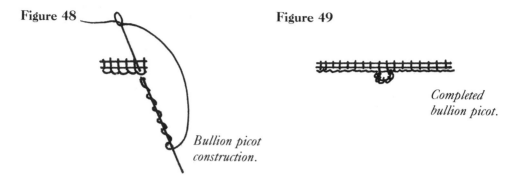

Figure 48

Figure 49

*Bullion picot
construction.*

*Completed
bullion picot.*

Picots for Bullion Projects

For *bullion* picots, insert your needle into the ridged part of the last buttonhole stitch as shown in figure 48. Then twist the working thread around the needle five times. Next, holding the twisted threads as snug as possible, pull the needle through. Make sure the next buttonhole stitch is worked snugly against the last, and the picot will look like the one in figure 49.

Picots for Buttonhole Projects

A *buttonholed* picot is by far the hardest and most time-consuming. A pin is used here, too, and the thread is placed under the head as before, then up and around the base threads of the bar and back under the pin head in the same direction as the first. Then insert the needle through the loops, as shown in figure 50, and pull tight. Now you can use a buttonhole stitch to cover the rest of the loop threads as shown in figure 51. The completed picot will look like the one in figure 52.

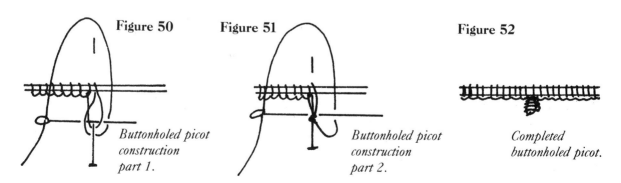

Figure 50

Figure 51

Figure 52

*Buttonholed picot
construction
part 1.*

*Buttonholed picot
construction
part 2.*

*Completed
buttonholed picot.*

Suggested Uses

* Table linens. This is where my love of cutwork originated because both of my grandmothers had beautiful cutwork tablecloths that they used on holidays at family dinners. One of these now belongs to my aunt (below), and the other to my mother (see page 20).

* Trim on clothing like the apron shown in figures 30 and 31. Cutwork also creates a striking effect when used on collars, cuffs, and the front pieces of a blouse.

* Individual quilt blocks

* Pillows

* Bellpulls (see figure 54)

Figure 53

Renaissance cutwork tablecloth belonging to my Aunt Phyllis Holmgren.

35

Detail of figure 53.

This bellpull hangs in my kitchen and is decorated with the simple cutwork design shown in figure 26.

Figure 54

Additional Patterns

The patterns shown in figures 26, 27, and 28 can be done entirely in buttonhole stitches.

I have explained earlier in this chapter that Renaissance and Richelieu patterns may be interchanged by the addition or deletion of the picots on the bars. Many of these same designs can be used as a simple form of cutwork with a few changes. Basically, cutwork patterns are versatile.

Instructions for Figures 55 and 56

To work the pattern shown in figures 55 and 56, use a satin stitch to complete the surface designs and a buttonhole stitch for the portions that are to be cut away. The picots are bullion picots. Since the design is more detailed, with smaller spaces than the ones described for the first pattern in this chapter, switch to size 8 Pearl Cotton for this pattern.

Instructions for Figures 57 and 58

The design shown in figures 57 and 58 is worked basically in buttonhole

Figure 55   *Details of Aunt Melanie Holmgren's Richelieu cutwork tablecloth. This pattern, which also has a lot of crocheted work on it, is one of my favorites.*

Figure 56

Pattern for Richelieu cutwork design shown in figure 55.

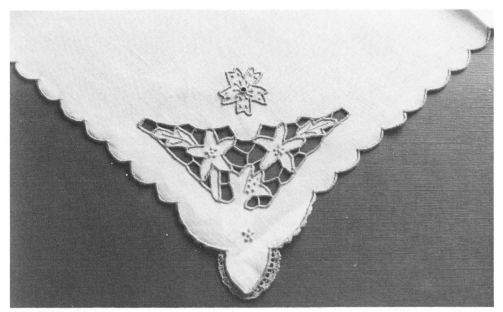

Figure 57

The corner of a dinner napkin done in Renaissance cutwork and decorated with stem and satin stitches.

Figure 58

Figure 59

Detail of Renaissance cutwork on the tablecloth pictured on page 20. This is the most difficult design in this chapter.

Figure 60

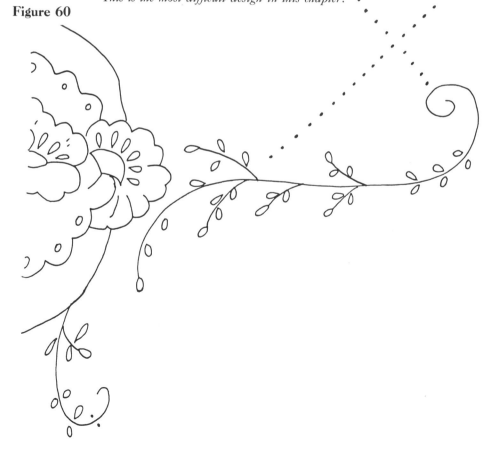

stitches including the bars. The exceptions are the stem-stitched designs on the leaves and the satin-stitched dots. Instead of size 5 Pearl Cotton, use size 8 on this pattern, too.

Instructions for Figures 59 and 60

The design worked in diagrams 59 and 60 is done in buttonhole stitches around the cutaway portions and the central flowers. The scrolled lines on the tablecloth pictured were done in a tiny satin stitch, but I would use a stem stitch to simplify it a bit.

My great-grandmother, Sarah Elizabeth
Litz Simmonds, wearing her cutwork collar.

3

HARDANGER EMBROIDERY

As my paternal blood runs strong down Norwegian and Swedish veins, I have been exposed to a great deal of sturdy Hardanger embroidery. This work can vary from fairly simple, with a lot of surface design, to highly intricate patterns with open fillet work.

Basic Hardanger is worked in groups of satin stitches, called kloster blocks, and various surface stitches depending on the pattern you are using. The klosters are grouped in geometric patterns on any even-count fabric in which the warp and weft threads are easily distinguished from one another. There is a special linen called Hardanger cloth made just for this type of work. It is medium price, comes in various widths and many colors. I prefer to use a cloth called Lugana which is available in white, ecru, and even a few colors. It is 54 inches wide and somewhat more expensive than Hardanger. This fabric washes beautifully, however, and requires minimal touch-up pressing. If you find a piece of fabric you like and wonder if it will work for Hardanger embroidery, count the number of threads in an inch both vertically and horizontally. If the counts are the same, the fabric will work fine. The cloth I use has 25 threads per inch. This is fairly standard, but if you have super eyesight, you can use less.

As it was originally done in Hardanger, Norway, only white thread on white linen or ecru thread on ecru linen was used, but today anything goes as far

Details of Hardanger embroidery
done on a checkered piece of linen fabric.

Figure 62

Mrs. Mary Ann Holman working on a tablecloth for her third child. Details of her sweepstakes-winning first tablecloth are shown in figure 78.

A hardanger sampler in progress.

as color is concerned. In doing this type of embroidery, you will hide the beginning and ending threads so the back side of the work looks as nice as the front. (One woman I spoke to told me about seeing a piece of work that was a State Fair sweepstakes winner displayed wrong-side forward!)

I have dresser scarves, tea towels, and placemats all decorated this way, some of them passed down from my grandmother, but the most beautiful piece of Hardanger I have seen is the luncheon cloth made by Mrs. Mary Ann Holman, which took sweepstakes in the needlework department at the Box Elder County Fair and first place at the Utah State Fair.

Figure 63   *Hardanger placemat.*

Figure 64   *Detail of placemat shown above.*

Supplies Needed

* Fabric for placemats. You will need a piece that measures 13 × 18 inches for each placemat, but buy a few extra inches to allow for the trimmed edges. Be sure the threads are easy to see as you will be counting them throughout the work. (You can get eight placemats from a yard of 54-inch-wide fabric if you cut them as shown in figure 66.)

* DMC Pearl Cotton size 5 (one ball does 1½ placemats)
* DMC Pearl Cotton size 8 (one ball does 12 placemats)
* Blunt darning needle size 20 (use with size 5 thread)
* Blunt darning needle size 24 (use with size 8 thread)
* Very sharp, pointed scissors

Construction

Remove a selvage from one side of your cloth by cutting ½ inch from the edge. (The selvages are woven tighter than the rest of the fabric, and run along the sides.) Be careful in doing this to follow a thread while cutting so your fabric will be "on the straight of grain" when you are finished. Figure 65 shows where the cuts are to be made for the first placemat. After removing the selvage, pull out a thread that runs perpendicular to the cut you just made and is close to the edge of the fabric; make the second cut along the line where the thread was removed. For cut number three, measure 18 inches from the second cut, and pull another thread for a guide; cut along this line. The fourth cut will be 13 inches from and run parallel to cut number one. You now have a piece of cloth that is 13 inches wide and 18 inches long. Cut each of the next pieces exactly the same size; make sure you follow the grain, as this will be the finished size of your placemats.

To get eight placemats from a yard of 54-inch-wide fabric, cut it as shown in figure 66, still carefully cutting along a thread line to keep the fabric straight. (This allows one extra inch that can be scrapped along the width.)

Thread the size 20 needle with a length of the size 5 thread, but do not make a knot in the end of the thread. Count in 20 threads from the left side of your placemat and 22 threads up from the bottom. This is the spot where

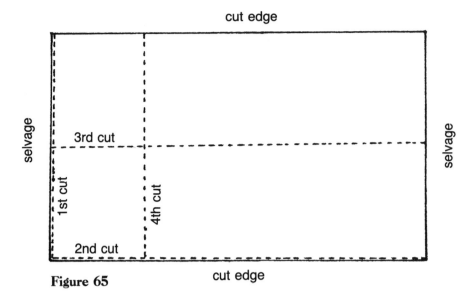

Figure 65

Fabric cutting directions.

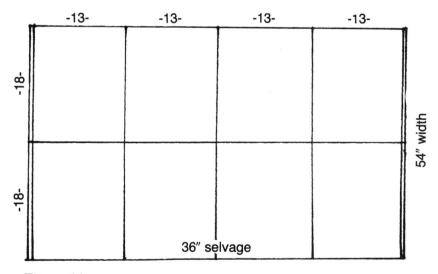

Figure 66

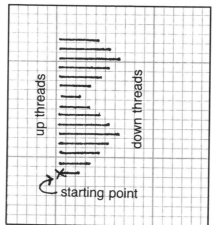

Figure 67 *Thread direction.*

you bring your needle up. Leave a 1-inch tail on the back side of the work. (You will surround this with satin stitches as you work the border.) To complete the first stitch, count two threads to the right on the same row, and take your needle down there. Come up one thread above the starting point. Count three threads to the right and go down again. See figure 67.

Bring the needle up one more thread above the starting point, and down four threads to the right. Bring the needle up again one thread above the last up stitch, and down five threads to the right. Come up one thread above the previous up stitch, and down six threads to the right. Continue bringing the needle up along the same line, and decrease the number of threads you move to the right by one each row to complete the triangular effect. The number of threads per inch your fabric has will determine how many points you will make along the left edge. The piece I worked on had 25 threads per inch, and I worked 35 points along this side. Count down 22 threads from the top, and make sure that your last triangle shape ends before or right on this point.

To complete the corner, work as illustrated in figure 68.

When you reach the starting corner, finish it as in figure 68, too, then take your needle through to the back side, run it under some of the stitches to catch it, and cut it off. This method keeps the back of the work looking as nice as the front.

Now remove the fabric threads that run perpendicular to the stitches along each edge. This leaves a fringed edge that is about 1 inch wide all the way around.

To make the interior designs, find the center point of the side edges. The

48

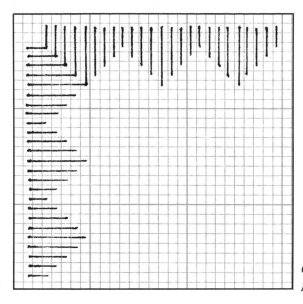

Figure 68

Corner design placement.

easiest way to do this is to count the number of little triangles that run along the side of the placemat and divide by two. If you had 35 triangles, the center point would be $17^1/_2$; the center point would therefore fall at the point of the 18th triangle. See figure 69.

From the edge of the fabric, count in 22 threads to begin making the klosters that will form the design. The starting point is marked on figure 70. Each kloster consists of five threads that run parallel to each other and cover four fabric threads.

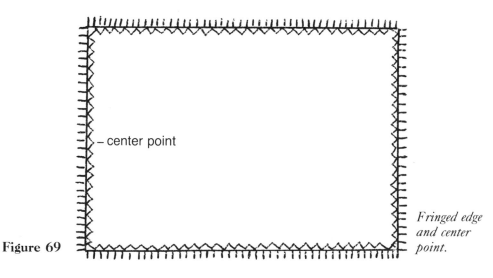

– center point

Figure 69

Fringed edge and center point.

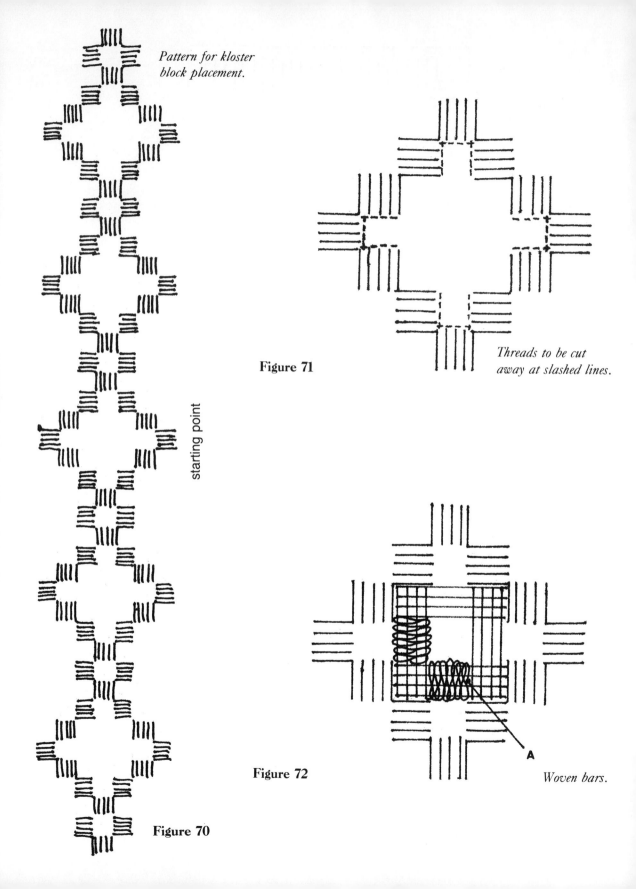

Pattern for kloster block placement.

Figure 71

Threads to be cut away at slashed lines.

starting point

Figure 72

Woven bars.

A

Figure 70

When you have finished the entire design as shown in figure 70, cut the fabric threads from the center of the designs as shown by the slashes on figure 71. Always cut the horizontal threads first, and remove them before doing the vertical ones, and be careful in cutting that you don't cut the pearl cotton, just the fabric threads.

To do the woven bars that form a square in the center of each cross, thread the size 24 needle with the size 8 thread. After running the needle under a few of the satin stitches to secure it, bring it up at point A (see figure 72), which is between the two middle threads.

Wrap the needle thread around the outside two fabric threads, and come back up again in the center. Wrap the needle thread this time around the inside two fabric threads, and again come back up in the center. Repeat the above until you have completely covered the four threads on that side of the square, then bring your needle up between the two center threads on the adjacent side. When you have covered three and a half sides of the inside square with this weaving stitch, do the lace filling by bringing your needle up in the center point of the first woven bar, shown as point B in figure 73.

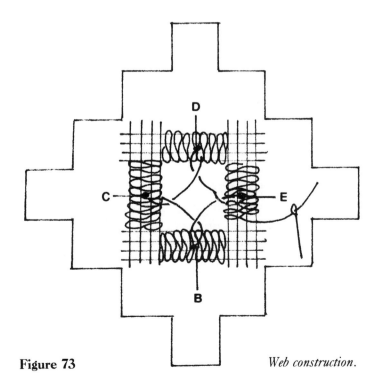

Figure 73   *Web construction.*

Before you bring your needle up through the center of the adjacent woven bar at point C, slip it *under* the B/E thread. Then before you come up at D, slip under the C/B thread. Finally, before coming up at E, go *over* the B/E thread, and then continue weaving the other half of the last bar. You have now formed what is called a web. Secure the thread on the back side and cut it off. Complete the center squares of the remainder of the design.

To finish, repeat this design on the other side of the placemat.

Finishing Techniques

To finish the placemat simply lay it face down on a towel and press lightly with a medium hot iron. To straighten the fringe, use a comb after the placemat has been set at the table.

Suggested Uses

* Table linens

* Dresser scarves

* Border design on clothing or curtains (see figure 82 for border pattern)

* Key holder

Additional Patterns

Instructions for Figures 74 and 75

The kloster blocks are five satin stitches over four threads. Work them first, and the single threads at the corners of the inside design. Cut the threads between the inside kloster blocks and complete the woven bars and web designs.

Instructions for Figures 76 and 77

Again, work the kloster blocks first, only on this pattern they will be seven satin stitches around six fabric threads (see figure 77). Complete the surface embroidered squares surrounding six fabric threads in both directions. Now cut the threads to be removed and work the woven bars and web designs.

Figure 74

This key holder is very simple to construct and makes a unique addition to a wall grouping.

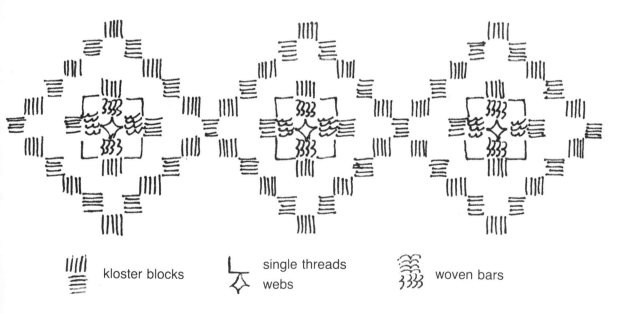

|||| kloster blocks   single threads   woven bars
                           webs

Figure 75

Figure 76

Details of small dresser scarf made by Mrs. Holman.

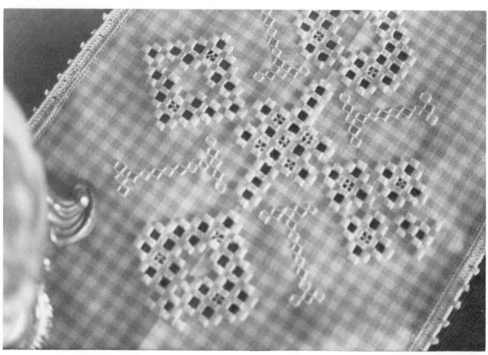

Figure 77

center line

center line

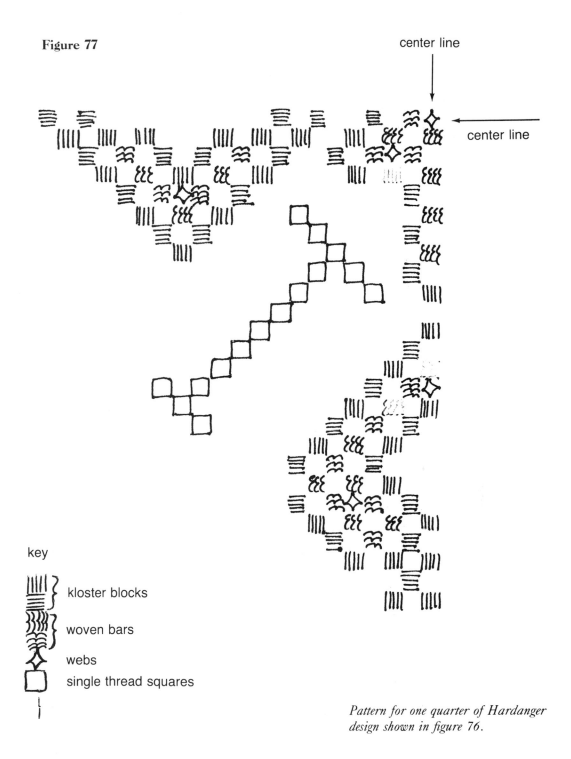

key

kloster blocks

woven bars

webs

single thread squares

Pattern for one quarter of Hardanger design shown in figure 76.

Instructions for Figures 78 and 79

There is quite a lot of cutwork done on this pattern with many woven bars and webs. It is not an extremely difficult pattern to work, but it is time-consuming. Work all of the kloster blocks first, using five satin stitches over four fabric threads as before. Next, do the surface embroidery work. The little squares (marked in figure 79 as A) are done by working over four fabric threads in both directions. The tulip-like flowers have 20 threads per side on each one and the little square at the top has nine threads.

When you have completed all the above, cut out the threads in the spaces shown in figure 78. Remember to cut and pull the horizontal threads and then the vertical ones. The bars are woven and the webs constructed, just like the ones on the placemat described at the beginning of this chapter.

Figure 78

Mrs. Mary Ann Holman's winning tablecloth, close up.

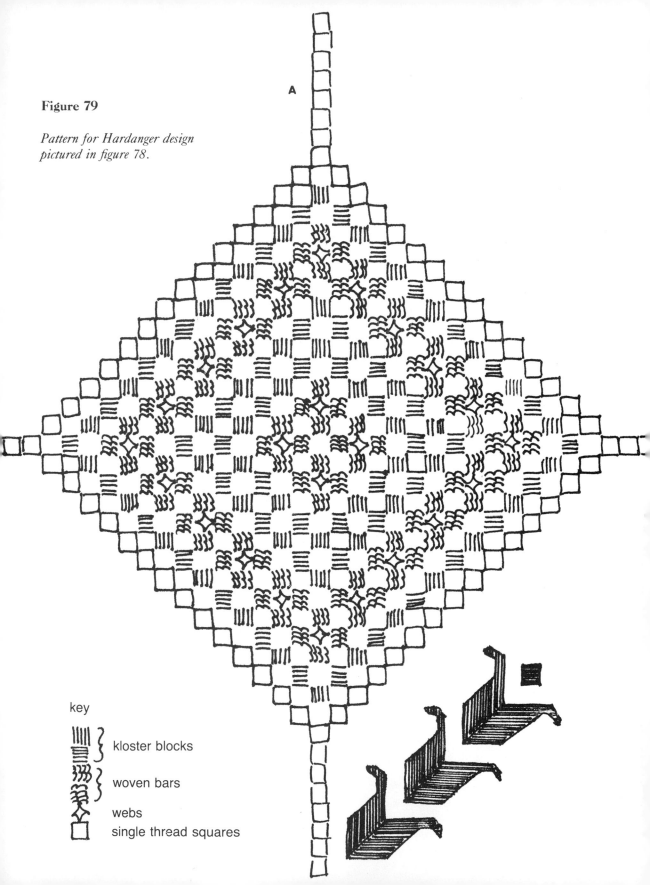

Figure 79

Pattern for Hardanger design pictured in figure 78.

A

key

)))) } kloster blocks

))) } woven bars

} webs

single thread squares

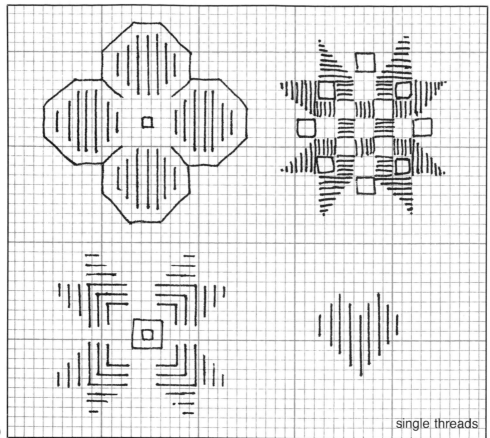

Figure 80

Figure 81   *Floral patterns for Hardanger worked together here on a gold pillow.*

Instructions for Figures 80 and 81

The patterns for some floral designs shown in figure 80 are most effective when they are worked in different colors. Figure 81 shows how some of them are worked.

Instructions for Figure 82

This design is simple. The kloster blocks are worked five satin stitches over four threads.

Figure 82

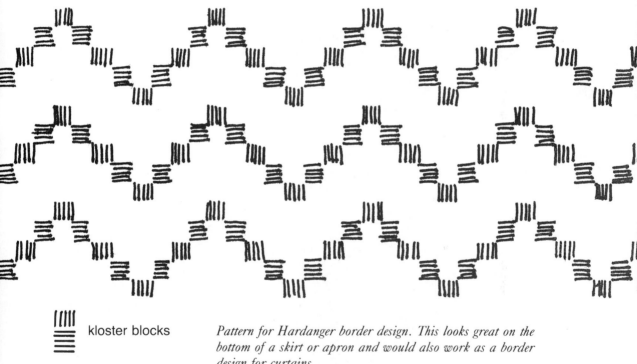

kloster blocks

Pattern for Hardanger border design. This looks great on the bottom of a skirt or apron and would also work as a border design for curtains.

4

HEDEBO

My maternal great-grandfather, James Hansen, left Aakerkeby, Born-holm, Denmark, for America in December 1853, and finally arrived in Salt Lake City, Utah, on October 5, 1854. His son, my grandfather, Isaac M. Hansen, was fluent in the Danish tongue, and along with an old hymn book and my Scandinavian complexion, he passed on to me an intense interest in Danish traditions, including the old lacemaking technique, Hedebo.

There are many machine-made laces that imitate this type of needlework, but the authentic handmade variety is rare today. Hedebo is Danish needle-point lace that is worked right on the edge of the fabric it is being used to decorate much like a crocheted edging, but a darning needle is used in the construction. It is one of the sturdiest of lace trims. Buttonhole and twisted buttonhole stitches are used exclusively, and picots are added on occasion to make the work look lacy. This technique can also be used as an inset and looks similiar to an Aemilia-ars lace motif (described in Chapter 1). In this case, though, the thread is worked right to the fabric while the pattern is formed and the designs can be any number of shapes, not just squares.

Earlier forms of Hedebo were done in the eighteenth century by peasants and consisted of surface work done in chain stitches with very little edge or openwork. Modern versions of Hedebo, however, are lacy and open in design.

This form of lace looks beautiful set into a collar or as a small design on

61

Towel edged with a sturdy hedebo lace pattern.

the front of a book cover, perhaps on an address book. One Christmas, my aunt sent a pair of bath towels trimmed with Hedebo done in a heavy thread. They add a unique and beautiful touch to my bathroom.

Supplies Needed

* Two towels
* Sharp darning needle size 16

* Coats & Clark's "Speed-Cro-Sheen" Mercerized Cotton
* Sharp scissors

Construction

To create this trim you must first form a row of foundation stitches along the edge of your towel. Use a buttonhole stitch to do this; however, the buttonhole stitch used for Hedebo is slightly different from the buttonhole stitch we have used previously in the book.

Hold the towel with the right side facing you and bring the needle up through the left corner. If your towel has a hemmed edge you can hide the knot inside the hem, but if it doesn't just make your knot as tiny as possible. Take the first stitch close to the left edge and about $1/4$ inch down from the top by bringing the needle through from the back. See figure 84.

Do not pull the thread tight at this point, but leave a loop at the top. To complete the stitch, bring your needle through the loop from the back again and then pull the thread tight with a small jerk away from the towel. Figure 85 illustrates how to do the second half of the buttonhole stitch as explained above.

If you find it necessary to rethread your needle, bring the needle up through the previous top loop and lay both the old and new threads toward the right. See figure 86. The next few stitches will be worked over both threads.

Continue working from left to right along the edge of the towel, spacing your stitches about $1/8$ of an inch apart. When you reach the right corner, come back across to the left side by overcasting each stitch along the top. See figure 87.

This will strengthen the foundation buttonhole stitches to make them last longer. When you reach the left corner again, secure and cut the thread.

Now start with a long thread at the right corner. Secure the thread tightly

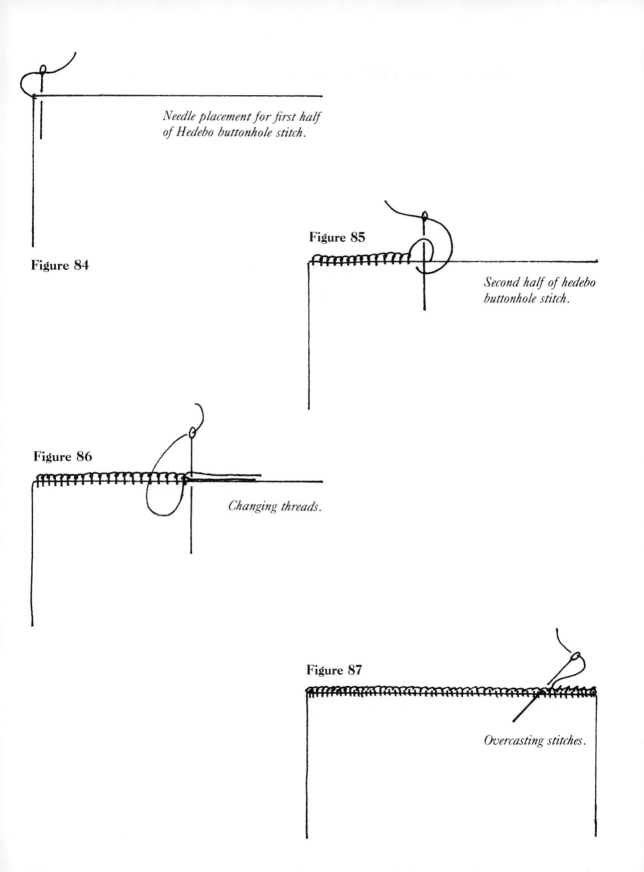

Needle placement for first half of Hedebo buttonhole stitch.

Figure 84

Figure 85

Second half of hedebo buttonhole stitch.

Figure 86

Changing threads.

Figure 87

Overcasting stitches.

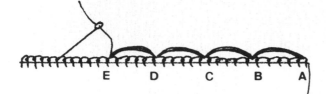

Laying the base threads.

Figure 88

Figure 89

Second row scallop.

Figure 90

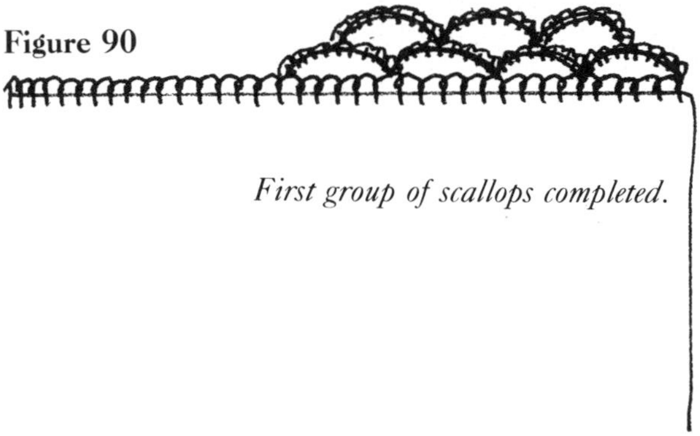

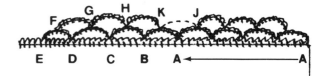

First group of scallops completed.

Attaching the second group of stitches to the first group.

Figure 91

to the towel, coming up at the top of the last foundation stitch at point A in figure 88. Count five stitches to the left (point B) and take your needle under the ridge formed by the foundation stitches. Go back to point A and catch the thread there, and then back again to point B. Leave a little slack in these stitches by not pulling them tight. This will form three base threads between point A and B. Now repeat the above procedure between B and C leaving three more base threads. Now lay your base threads between C and D, and then between D and E. You will have formed four loops of three base threads each.

At this point, start working toward the right again by covering the three base threads with the same buttonhole stitch that you used as a foundation stitch. Cover the space from E to D, and halfway across the space between D and C to G (see figure 89). Then take the thread back and catch it at F. Then to G, then F again. This will form the base threads for a second row scallop. Work buttonhole stitches over the base threads between F and G, then finish the second half of the D/C scallop. Work to point H and use the same method to make the three base threads for the scallop between H and G.

When you reach point A again your edging should look like figure 90. Secure the thread by running it back under a few of the buttonhole stitches and cut it off.

Now what was point E becomes point A, and you build your second set of scallops in this row. See figure 91. This time, however, when you get back to point A, don't secure or cut the thread. Top sew (overcast, as illustrated in figure 87) along the edge of the last scallop from the previous group to the halfway point, and lay three base threads between J and K. (See dotted line in figure 91.) Buttonhole stitch over these threads from K back to J and then secure and cut the thread.

By doing this you form the scallop that joins the second row.

Once again, start with a new thread and continue across by working these groups of scallops. When you get close to the left edge of the towel again you will probably have to work a smaller bunch of scallops in the last group to make the design end flush with the side of the towel.

Finishing Techniques

Cover an ironing board with a thick towel and lay the edge of your article face down on top of it. See figure 92. Secure the pattern with pins to hold its shape.

Spray lightly with spray starch, and cover with a damp press cloth. With your iron at a medium hot setting (cotton), press down on the Hedebo edging; be careful to lift and lower the iron each time and not slide it. When the press cloth has been ironed dry, remove it and let the Hedebo edge air dry overnight with the pins still in place.

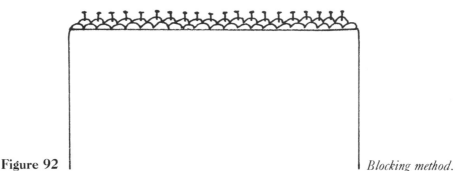

Figure 92 | *Blocking method.*

Finished edge. Detail of towel pictured on page 60.

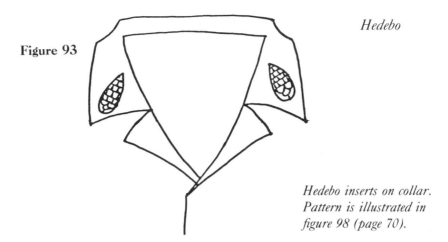

Figure 93

Hedebo

Hedebo inserts on collar. Pattern is illustrated in figure 98 (page 70).

Suggested Uses

* Trim the ends of a table runner

* Trim the ends of placemats or napkin corners

* Insert on a collar or cuff

* Quilt blocks

* Hand-washable blouses

* Insert for book cover or a case for eyeglasses (see figure 94)

Additional Patterns

Instructions for Figure 95
Work this pattern (figure 95) just like the one described at the beginning of this chapter, but vary the length of the base threads to achieve the different-sized scallops and disregard the instructions for the second row.

Instructions for Figure 96
Work this pattern (figure 96) by laying and covering the base threads of the larger scallops on the bottom row first, and then treating the second row totally separate starting from the right side again.

Instructions for Figure 97
The first two rows of scallops in figure 97 are worked exactly like the

Figure 94   *Hedebo insert on book cover. Pattern is shown in figure 100 (page 70).*

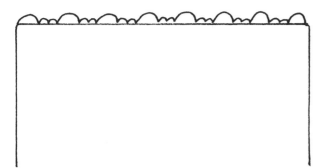

Figure 95

*Hedebo edging pattern with scallops in varied sizes.
Could be used on a table runner or placemat.*

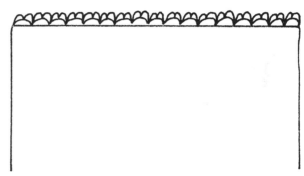

Figure 96

*Hedebo edging pattern with large scallops on first
row, topped by small scallops. Done in a
lightweight thread, this would work well on a
handkerchief or even clothing.*

Figure 97

*This Hedebo pattern is like the one explained
previously for the towel, with two more rows.*

Figure 98

Pattern for Hedebo insert pictured on a collar in figure 93.

Figure 99

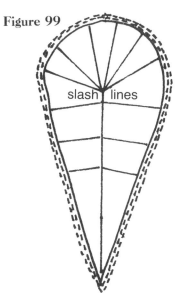

slash lines

Cutting lines for the collar insert pattern.

Figure 100

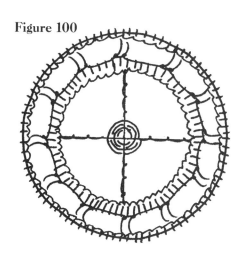

Pattern for Hedebo insert on the book cover shown in figure 94.

Figure 101

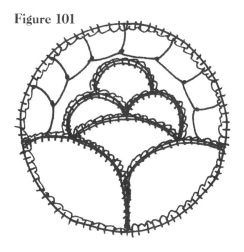

Pattern for Hedebo insert. This would look neat on a pocket.

pattern described at the beginning of this chapter. Then start at point A, as marked in figure 97, and work two more rows in the same way.

Instructions for Figures 93, 98, and 99

To work the design shown in figures 93 and 98, trace the pattern and slash marks shown in figure 99 onto the collar. Make two rows of running stitches around the outside edge.

Cut along the slash lines and fold the cut fabric back under the uncut fabric. Using DMC Pearl Cotton (size 8), make Hedebo buttonhole stitches outlining the edge of the design. Work through both layers of fabric. When you have completely outlined the design in buttonhole stitches, turn to the back and trim the extra fabric close to the stitches.

Work the bricked-like effect from the point, in loose buttonhole stitches whipping back to the left side along the top of each row. The top row is done in close buttonhole stitches, and then the scallops from right to left as explained earlier in the chapter.

Instructions for Figures 94 and 100

The pattern shown in figures 94 and 100 is worked like the one described for figure 98. The inside cross is twisted bars with a woven center. To make this, lay the base thread for the bar and twist the thread around to the other side. To weave the center, go over and under each bar in turn to achieve the effect shown in figure 100.

Instructions for Figure 101

Work the outside edge of the pattern shown in figure 101 like the one described in figure 98. Work the lower three scallops together, the top three scallops next, and, finally, the loose buttonhole stitches around the top half.

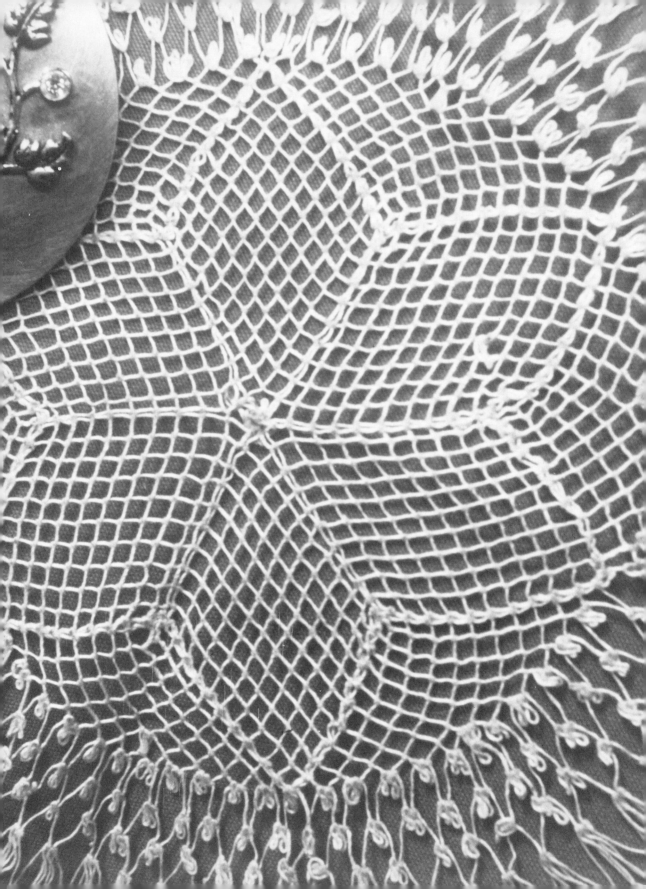

5

NETTING

In its simplest form, netting looks like a fishnet, and, in fact, the same technique is used for both. Netting is done by wrapping the thread around your hand, weaving the netting needle through the wrap, and then tightening the thread in the proper way to form a knot. Of all the techniques covered in this book, netting is probably the oldest and the rarest today. Many figures found on the Egyptian tombs are shown wearing tunics which were netted, but then it was called caul work. In Homer's *Iliad*, the Trojan women wore cauls of gold. The prophet Isaiah talks about the cauls of network worn by the Jewish women. In all my research, I found only one book that went into any detail at all on this form of needlework. The book, *Dictionary of Needlework* by S. F. A. Caulfeild, was in the historical archive at Utah State University and had been published in England in 1887. In it, the author states that the best netting needle to use is made of bone. I've had a hard enough time finding retail outlets for the metal variety (see supply information on page 153) so I think I'll pass on trying to track down the bone model.

Even in the area where I grew up, where needlework talents are abundant, I could only find a handful of women who even knew what a netting needle was, and only one who could teach me the art. To Agnes Bishop I am indebted for her patience while my fingers learned to keep the right tensions on the thread and when to release it to complete the knots. Netting is one of the

Netted doily.

Netted doilies done by Mrs. Agnes Bishop and her mother. The gold watch has been passed down through seven generations to the oldest daughter, and the quilt was made sometime in the late 1700s.

Figure 102

Figure 103

Mrs. Anges Bishop instructs her daugher Phyllis Holmgren, her granddaughter Clixie Hollingsworth, and her great-granddaughter Tanna Hollingsworth in the technique of netting.

many things that have been passed from mother to daughter in Mrs. Bishop's family—along with an antique watch, some first edition books, and a quilt made by her great-grandmother Jardine in the late 1700s (figure 102). In figure 103 she has been photographed instructing three more generations of her family in the art of netting.

Once you have mastered the knot, you have learned to net, but don't get too excited yet, because it takes a lot of practice to get the feel of it. I watched the procedure once and thought it was extremely simple. What a misconception! When I tried it the first time, I felt I was entangled in thread and that I needed at least three more hands. I worked for a full half hour before I finally got one knot right. When I finished jumping up and down, I realized that Mrs. Bishop had finished the last two rows of an 18-inch doily in the same amount of time. She assured me that speed would come with practice.

To begin learning, it is easiest to net along the edge of a handkerchief until you feel comfortable with the knotting technique and can keep your loops very even and uniform. A handkerchief edging or a doily done in netting can become a rare treasure almost immediately because there are few people who know or even recognize the technique.

Supplies Needed

* Netting needle
* Long crewel needle
* Knitting needle size 5 (to be used as a mesh stick)
* Handkerchief that has been hemstitched

* Size 100 thread is used for the most delicate effect, but with a courser thread you will be able to see the knots a little more clearly

Construction

Thread the darning needle with a medium length of thread, about 18 to 20 inches. Secure this thread to the left-hand corner of one edge of the handkerchief by passing it through a hemstitch hole and then tying a square knot. This is obviously the easy part.

Fasten the handkerchief to something so you can hold it snug while working. I pin it right to my jeans just above the knee, but if you prefer you can use the arm of an upholstered chair.

Figure 104

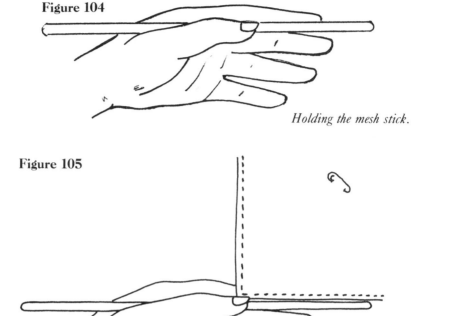

Holding the mesh stick.

Figure 105

Handkerchief edge placed along mesh stick and secured with a safety pin.

Hold the mesh stick (knitting needle in this case) in your left hand with the length running in front of your pointer finger and along the top of the middle finger. Your thumb rests over the top as illustrated in figure 104.

This may feel awkward at first, but it's like riding a bicycle; once you get the feel of it, you're on your way. Hold the handkerchief in front of the pointer finger, so that its edge runs along the top of the mesh stick. See figure 105. You won't need to worry about holding the handkerchief with either hand, because once you start wrapping the thread, it is held by the loops.

To tie the first knot, bring the thread in front of the mesh stick, down and around the middle and fourth fingers, then back up behind the same two fingers and the mesh stick. Now bring the thread in front of the handkerchief and hold it to the left against the mesh stick with the thumb as shown in figures 106 and 107.

To continue the wrapping motion, throw the thread away from you and

76

Figure 106

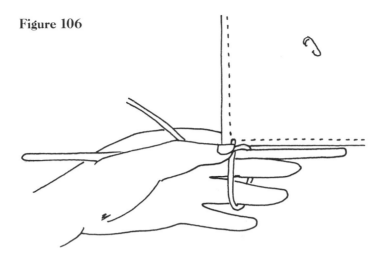

First half of wrap.

Figure 107

Figure 108

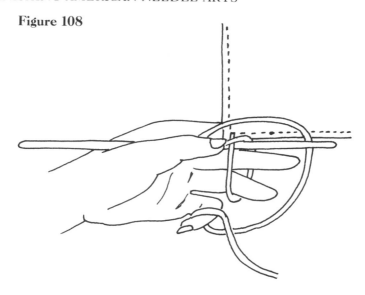

Second half of wrap.

Figure 109

back to the right, leaving a loop and coming back down behind the mesh stick. Now wrap it around the little finger from back to front. The wrapping is completed at this point and should look like the examples in figures 108 and 109.

To begin passing the needle through the wrapping, take it first in front of the two middle fingers to the right of the thread. Next take the needle behind the mesh stick and come up through the back side of the handkerchief two hemstitch holes to the right. The needle should come in front of the thread forming the top loop. See figures 110 and 111.

Keeping the thread wrapped, pull the needle through and tighten the thread by pulling it toward you, as illustrated in figure 112.

Let go of the thread under your thumb and tighten again. See figure 113.

To hold the stitch stable, move your thumb over to cover it now. See figure 114.

At this point, slip the middle two fingers from their loop and pull the thread tight again. To make sure it is snug, work it back and forth a little with the loop held by the little finger. When this stage of the knot is tight you should see the knot come from behind to the top of the mesh stick and wrapped over the needle thread you are pulling. See figures 115 and 116.

Now release the loop held by the little finger and pull the thread tight. The knot is complete and you should have one loop around your mesh stick. See figure 117.

The whole trick to netting is releasing the wrapped threads in the proper order and keeping the needle thread tension right.

Continue along the handkerchief edge by repeating the above knot until you reach the right-hand corner. To round the corner, make three knots in the corner hole, and then pull the mesh stick out of all of the loops. Insert it again in the last loop formed and continue forming knots along the next edge of the handkerchief as illustrated in figure 118.

When you have formed the loops on all four sides, make sure there are three loops in the starting corner and cut the thread.

Now wind the thread around the netting needle taking care not to wind too much; the needle must pass through the loops of thread easily.

Leave a ¼″ tail of thread on the end; it won't show on the finished article. Tie the end of this thread to the starting loop of the first edge of the handkerchief and net as above coming up through each loop of the first row instead of the hemstitched holes. It is a little more difficult to keep the stitches even in this row, but if you are careful to tighten the knots to the top of the mesh stick, it will be easier. See figures 119 and 120.

Figure 110

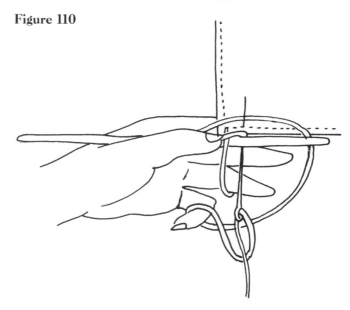

Inserting the needle through the wrapped threads.

Figure 111

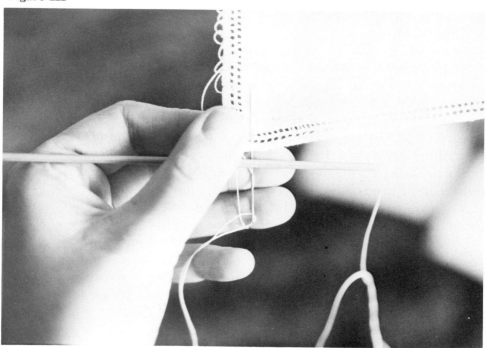

Figure 112

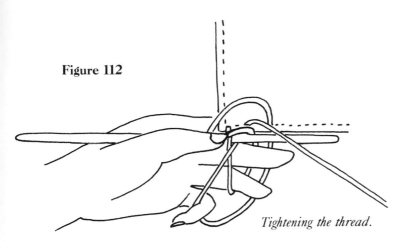

Tightening the thread.

Figure 113

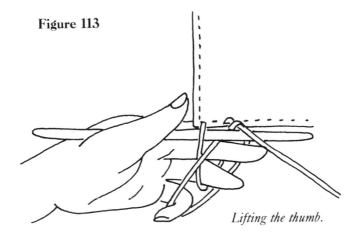

Lifting the thumb.

Figure 114

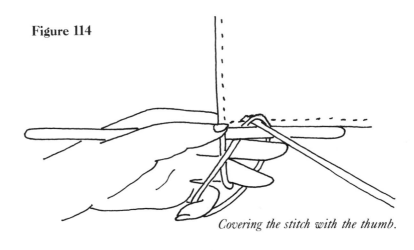

Covering the stitch with the thumb.

Figure 115

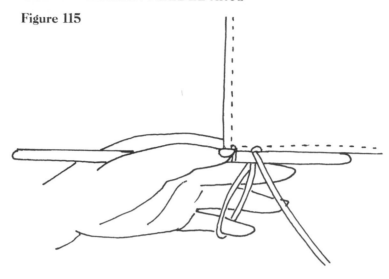

*Dropping the loop from
the middle fingers.*

Figure 116

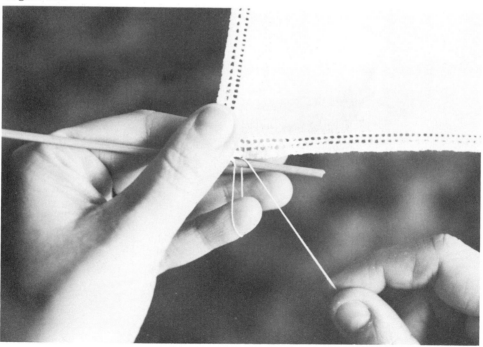

Figure 117

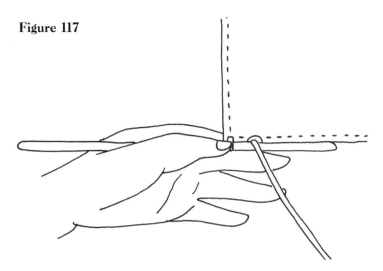

*Dropping the thread from the
little finger and tightening the knot.*

Figure 118

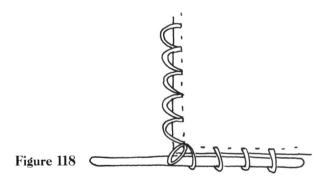

Corner stitches.

Figure 119

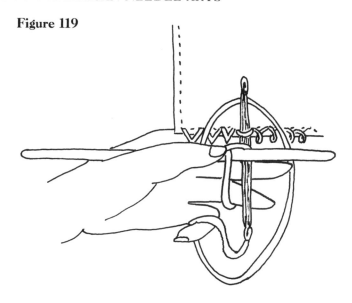

Second row stitch construction.

Figure 120

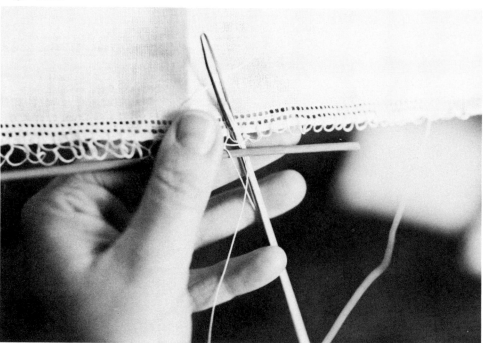

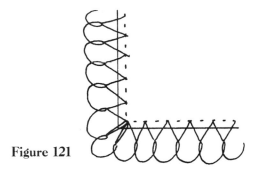

Figure 121

Corner stitches.

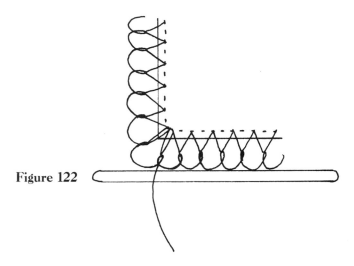

Figure 122

Starting row three.

Make three knots in each of the corner loops as shown in figure 121.

When you have completed the second round, don't cut the thread. Just pull the mesh stick out and start row three, leaving enough thread to bring it down to the next row. See figure 122.

Work row four in the same manner as row three.

When you find it necessary to start a new thread in the middle of a row, tie the new thread to the old one in a square knot, close to the last knot that was formed, and trim the ends.

Finishing Techniques

To finish the edge of the handkerchief, lay it on your ironing board and pull the edging out to look like figure 123.

Using the side of your iron, slide it from the handkerchief outward, pressing the edge into place. Then lay a strip of waxed paper over the netting, cover that with a thin, dry press cloth and press again. Carefully lift and lower the iron so you don't slide the netting.

If you want your edging to be stiffer, you can use spray starch to keep it blocked, but be very careful not to overstarch it.

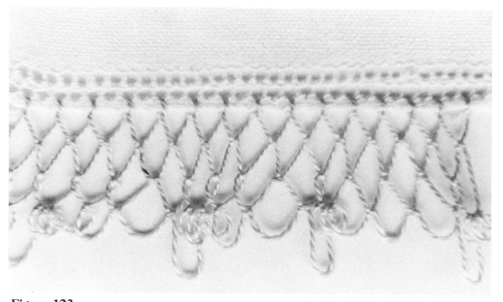

Figure 123

Blocking.

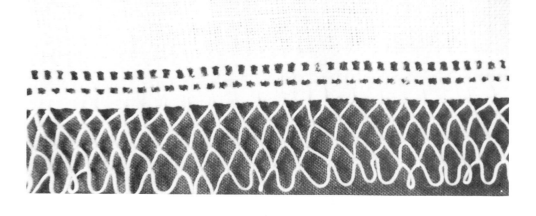

Suggested Uses

* Trim for pillowcases

* Trim for collars or cuffs

* Trim for scarves or dresser scarves

* Trim for a linen doily

* Trim for evening clothes and lingerie

Additional Patterns

Some of these patterns have been passed down for generations and figure 125 shows the rough manner in which they were jotted down. The paper is cracked and yellowed, but the tradition is carried on with the threads.

Instructions for Figure 124

Net plain over a size 5 knitting needle except on rows four and seven. For these rows you use the stitch variation explained below (see figure 124).

About every 14 loops, you form the little heartlike shapes by netting three loops in one loop and three loops in the next loop. This forms the top part of the heart. To form the point, catch all six loops in one loop on the fifth and eighth rows.

The hearts on the seventh row are spaced in between the hearts on the fourth row.

Net plain on the last four rows.

Figure 124

Netted handkerchief edgings done by Mrs. Agnes Bishop.

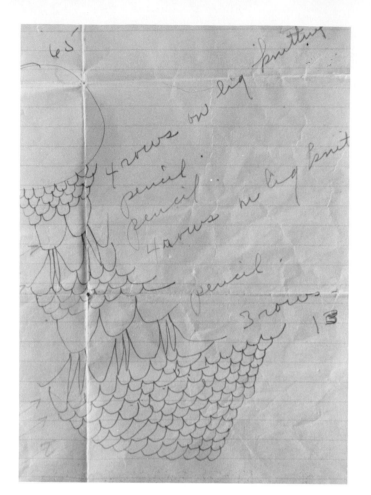

Figure 125

Old pattern handwritten and passed down to Mrs. Mary Gardner by her mother.

Figure 126

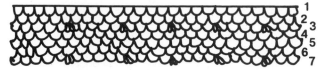

This netted edging, done in a heavy thread, would look nice on towels.

Figure 127

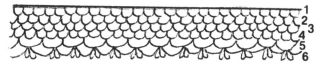

Netted edging that would look especially nice on a collar.

Figure 128

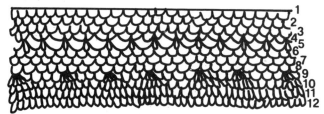

A linen doily would be enhanced by this netted edging.

Figure 129

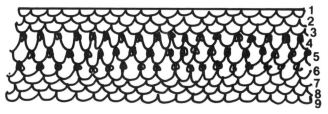

A pillowcase edged with this netting would be nice.

Instructions for Figure 126

Net two rows plain over size 5 knitting needle (see figure 126).

For the third row, net three plain and then net three knots in the fourth loop. Net three plain and then net three knots in the eighth loop. Continue this pattern all the way around the third row.

On the fourth row, net plain and when you come to the three loops together, catch all three of them in one knot.

Net two rows plain.

For the seventh row, repeat row three.

Instructions for Figure 127

Net four rows plain over a size 5 knitting needle (see figure 127).

Net the fifth row into every other loop over a size 7 knitting needle.

Net the sixth row over the size 7 knitting needle also, making three loops in each loop of the previous row.

Instructions for Figure 128

Net plain over a size 3 knitting needle for the first three rows (figure 128).

Net row four over a size 5 knitting needle.

For row five, use the size 5 knitting needle again, and net two of the loops of the previous row into the same loop and then net one more loop in the same loop. Continue this all the way around, remembering to add stitches at the corner so the edging will lay flat.

For rows six, seven, and eight, net plain over a size 3 knitting needle.

Row nine is done by netting four in the first loop, then netting the next three loops plain. Repeat this for the entire row using a size 5 knitting needle.

Net plain for rows 10, 11, and 12 over a size 3 knitting needle.

Instructions for Figure 129

Net rows 1, 2, and 3 plain over a size 3 knitting needle (see figure 129).

For rows 4, 5, and 6 use a knot stitch, which consists of wrapping the thread around the mesh stick twice before you make the loop. This will make your loop twice as long. To complete the knot stitch, net two more loops into the same loop. On the next row, net only into the long loop.

Rows 7, 8, and 9 are netted plain.

6

SMOCKING

Smocking originated way back when heavy fabrics had to be gathered for mobility of garment, and a desire to ornament the effect was wanted also. I haven't been able to locate an exact date or place, because several countries have used the methods described here for many generations.

The basics of this technique are simple and the results are beautiful, particularly when different patterns are combined in rows. Three separate types of smocking are covered in this chapter. In the first, regular smocking, or honeycombing, the fabric is drawn together from the right side. In English smocking, the fabric is gathered into tiny, even pleats, and decorative stitches are used to anchor them. The third type, lattice smocking, is worked from the wrong side of the fabric and creates a woven effect.

I have used smocking on articles of clothing for years. The work is not difficult to do, but takes a bit of time. Most people would rather run machine gathers and for this reason smocking is becoming a vanishing art.

Smocking has traditionally been most used on babies' and children's clothing, but women's lingerie looks very delicate trimmed this way. The Hungarians use smocking on their national costumes. Decorative pillows or tiny sachets also look great when they are smocked.

Antique china doll owned by Mrs. Lota Brinton, who did the English smocking on the dress and bonnet.

Figure 131

Lattice and honeycomb smocked pillows in a grouping.

Regular Smocking

Supplies Needed

* Ruler for marking dots
* Number two pencil to mark the fabric, or a lighter pencil that will show up on your particular fabric color
* A sharp needle size 26
* DMC Pearl Cotton size 8 (this can be a contrasting color or can match your fabric)

* Fabric (It is easiest to learn using a solid color; an 18-inch square piece of lightweight fabric is good)
* Sharp scissors

Construction

Leaving a one-inch border all around, mark tiny dots on the right side of your fabric $1/4$ inch apart. See figure 132. These dots must run exactly horizontal and perpendicular to each other to make the finished work even.

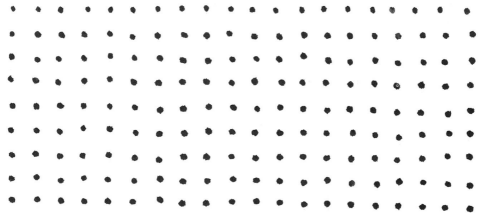

Figure 132   *Dots for regular or honeycomb smocking.*

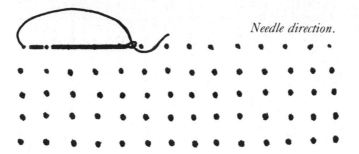

Needle direction.

Figure 133

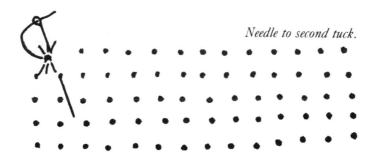

Needle to second tuck.

Figure 134

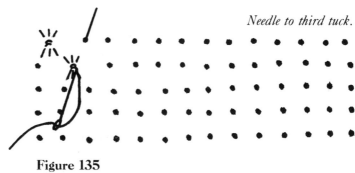

Needle to third tuck.

Figure 135

A little girl at the piano wearing her Smocked pinafore.

Teneriffe hotpad.

Various Teneriffe designs and colors.

With your needle threaded, come up from the back of the fabric through the top left dot leaving a tiny knot on the back to secure the thread. Now take a tiny stitch in the next dot to the right. See figure 133.

Take another stitch at the first dot where the thread came up and pull the thread tight forming a tiny tuck. Push your needle down at this tuck and up into the second dot from the left on the second row. See figure 134. (Don't pull it tight here, but leave enough thread running along the back of the fabric to reach the second row.)

Take a little stitch one dot to the left again, and then another back at the dot where the thread is coming up now. Pull the thread tight to form tuck number two. The needle will go down by this tuck and back up to the next dot on row one as shown in figure 135.

Continue to the right side of the fabric working rows one and two at the same time, as described above. Knot and cut the thread. Then come back to the dot at the extreme left end of row three to start the next rows.

When you have finished a few rows you will be able to see the honeycomb effect created by this type of smocking. See figure 136.

Figure 136   *Details of regular smocking.*

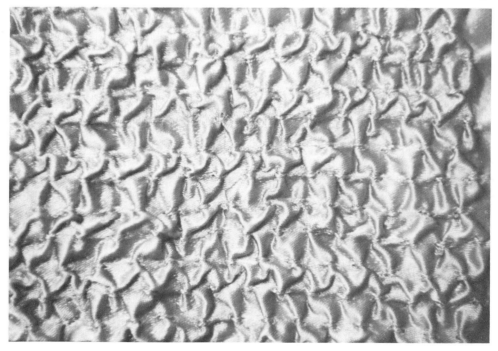

97

Lattice and honeycomb Smocked pillows.

English Smocking

Supplies Needed

* A sharp darning needle size 26

* Three colors DMC Pearl Cotton size 8

* Fabric. The easiest way to do this type of smocking is to have your fabric prepleated on a Durand Pleater. If you don't know a needlework supply outlet that provides this service locally, check the Yellow Pages under Needlework Supplies and call a few places. Frequently, if one place does not provide the service, they can refer you to someone who does. If you still can't locate the service near you, you can send your fabric to ZeAnn's Needlework Supplies, 3692 South 4225 West, West Valley City, UT 84120. Note how many rows (up to 24) you would like gathered. You may also order fabric in some colors from her, but specify that you want it pleated for English smocking. It will cost approximately $3.50 if you want a full 24 rows of fabric pleated. The fabric costs are over and above this; send for a list of fabric prices.

Construction

Secure the gathering threads left by the pleater, on both sides by knotting with a slip knot. Tie the top thread by itself, and the rest in groups of three.

To set the pleats in your fabric, use a mist sprayer to spray it lightly with water, making sure the pleats are pushed together tightly. Leave the fabric to dry for eight to twelve hours and the pleats will have a more definite crease and be easier to work with.

Figure 137 shows the complete pattern of stitches you will be using. For this project you will need 17 pleated rows.

Thread your needle with a medium length of thread and make a small knot at the end. Bring the needle up to the left side of the first pleat on the second row. Throw your thread away from you and take a stitch through the first pleat right along the gathering thread line as shown in figure 138.

Figure 137

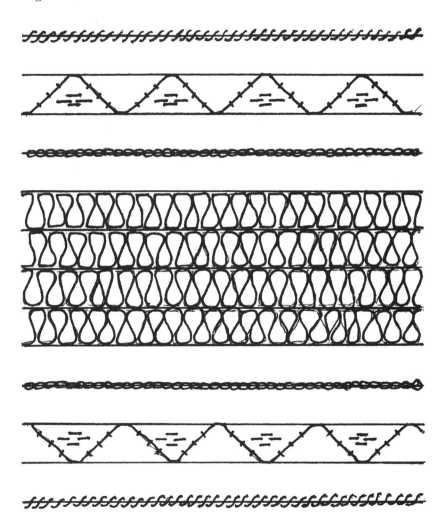

English smocking pattern.

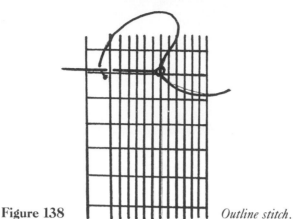

Figure 138   *Outline stitch.*

Repeat this (outline) stitch toward the right in each pleat.

To start the trellis stitch, move down two rows of gathering threads and come up as before to the left of the first pleat. Throw the thread toward you and take a stitch through the second pleat. Still throwing your thread toward you, stitch through the third pleat a quarter of the width toward the row above. Stitch three will be halfway to the row above, stitch four, three-quarters, etc. See figure 139.

Take stitch five right on the row above where you started, but this time throw the thread away from you.

Come down the other side of the triangle shape by throwing your thread away from you and lining the stitches up with those on the first side. See figure 140.

Figure 139   **Figure 140**

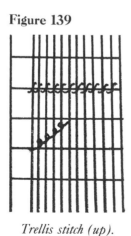   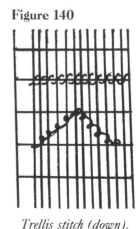

Trellis stitch (up).   *Trellis stitch (down).*

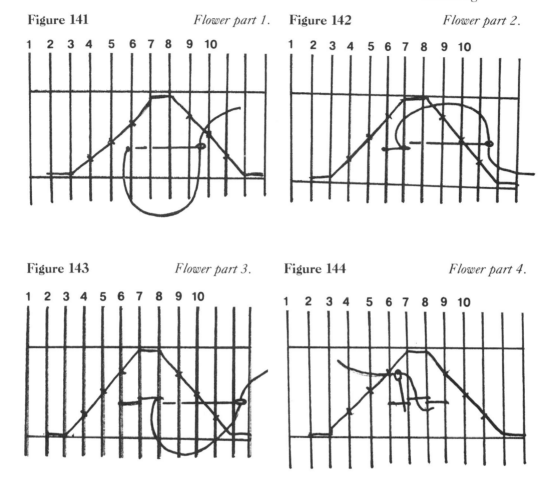

Figure 141   *Flower part 1.*   **Figure 142**   *Flower part 2.*

Figure 143   *Flower part 3.*   **Figure 144**   *Flower part 4.*

At the bottom change the direction you throw your thread and start again, continuing this stitch to the other side of the fabric.

To insert the little flowers, come up to the left of the sixth pleat and, throwing your thread down, take a stitch through the seventh pleat. See figure 141.

Now throw the thread up and take a stitch through the eighth pleat just barely above the previous stitch. See figure 142.

Next, with the thread down, take a stitch through the ninth pleat at the same level as the first stitch. See figure 143.

The last stitch is worked by taking the needle down between the sixth and seventh pleats. See figure 144.

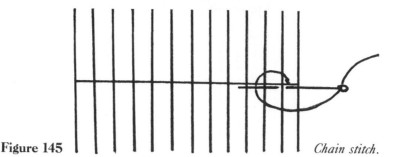

Figure 145 *Chain stitch.*

Work flowers in each of the triangle shapes by coming up two pleats from the left base.

To do the next row, which is worked in chain stitches, bring your needle up on the other side of the fabric to the right of the last pleat, one row below the trellis design. Throw your thread away from you and then back toward the left, forming a loop. Now take a stitch through the pleat, keeping the needle above the thread. See figure 145.

Continue this stitch to the left side of the fabric, stitching through each pleat individually.

The next row of stitches is done in what is called the Van Dyke stitch. Again you start on the right side of the fabric coming up to the left side of the last pleat, two rows below the chain-stitch row. Next take a stitch through two pleats. Throw your thread away from you and stitch again through the same two pleats. See figure 146.

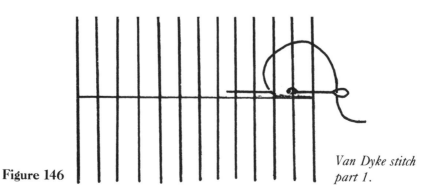

Figure 146 *Van Dyke stitch part 1.*

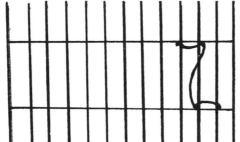

Figure 147

*Van Dyke stitch
part 2.*

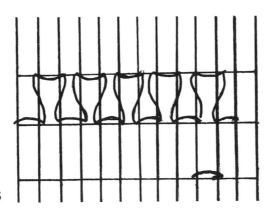

Figure 148

*Starting the second row
of Van Dyke stitches.*

Now move up to the next row and take a stitch through two pleats—one used on the previous stitch, and the other a new one. Throw the thread toward you and stitch again through these two pleats. See figure 147.

Complete this stitch across to the left side by continuing in the manner described above.

Start the next row of Van Dyke stitches one row down, but come up to the left side of the second pleat instead of the first. See figure 148.

The third row is just like the first row of Van Dyke stitches, and the fourth row is done like the second one.

After completing the Van Dyke group, skip down a row and do another row of chain stitches.

The trellis stitches on the next row are reversed directions from the ones previously done. Just remember that when you are moving down the work

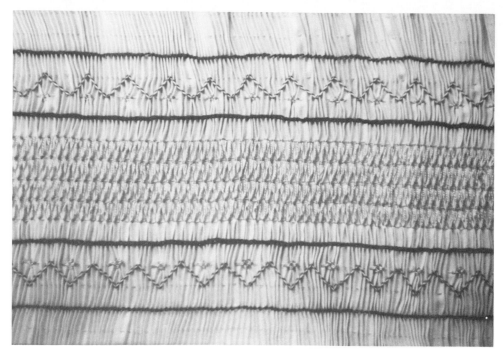

Figure 149   *English smocking close-up.*

you throw your thread away from you, and when you are moving up you throw the thread toward you.

Complete the flowers inside the trellis stitches.

One more row of outline stitches completes the work. See figure 149.

Lattice Smocking

Supplies Needed

* Sharp needle size 26
* Heavy buttonhole thread
* Ruler for marking dots

* Marker
* Fabric, $1/2$ yard (velvet is most effective, but a heavy satin will work, too)

Construction

Dots are marked as in figure 150, on the wrong side of the fabric.

On the first piece of work it might help you to number each of the dots right on the fabric.

Take a tiny stitch at number 1 (see figure 151) to secure the thread. Next take a stitch at 2 and then one more at 1, pulling the thread tight to create a tuck.

Move the needle down to 3 and take a stitch there. To secure the thread so it will not pull tight between 2 and 3, knot the thread by running the needle under the 2/3 thread and over the needle thread as shown in figure 151.

Now take a stitch at 4, then back to 3 and pull the thread tight to create another tuck. Continue down the fabric taking tucks between the stitches indicated by the slashes on the pattern in figure 150.

When you complete the first row of tucks, end the thread and start a new one. Move to the top of the fabric and complete each row in the same vertical pattern. You will soon be able to see the pattern forming on the right side of the fabric. See figure 152.

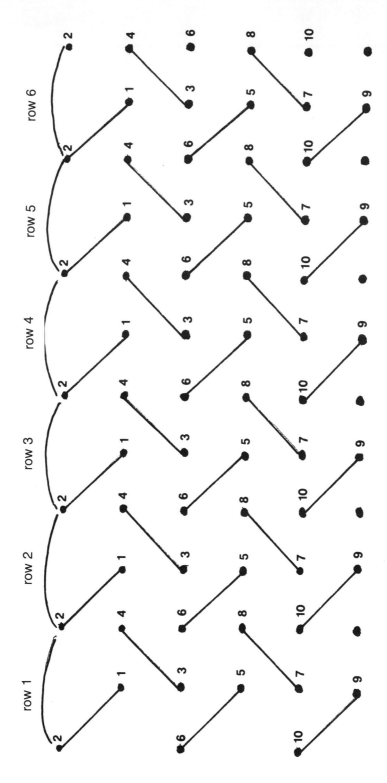

Figure 150

*Pattern for
lattice smocking.*

Figure 151

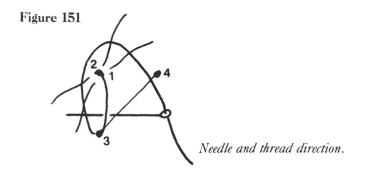

Needle and thread direction.

Figure 152   *Lattice smocking close-up.*

Finishing Techniques

Use a row of tucks for a seam line as shown in figures 153, 154, and 155. For regular and lattice smocking, you can leave an unsmocked border to use in construction, also making your finished piece larger.

In English smocking, once you have finished, remember to remove the gathering threads.

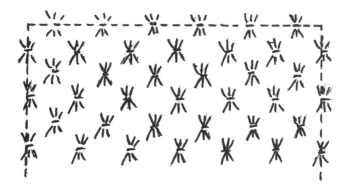

Figure 153   *Seam line placement for regular smocking.*

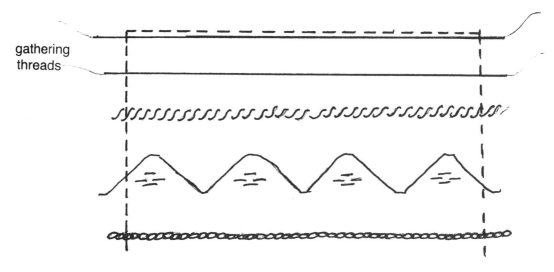

Figure 154   *Seam line placement for English smocking.*

Figure 155   *Seam line placement for lattice smocking.*

Suggested Uses

* Clothing
* Sachets
* Pillows
* Handbags
* Curtains
* Doll clothes

Additional Patterns

Additional patterns are not given for regular and lattice smocking because they don't vary. Although the patterns are always the same, you may change the look by placing the smocking in different positions on a garment, for example, at the top of a sleeve, on the yoke of a blouse, or at the waistline of a dress. You can also smock only a portion of an item like the middle of a pillow or the top of a handbag to get a different look.

The stitches used in figures 156 through 159 are the same ones shown previously in the chapter. The placement of the stitches has been changed in each diagram to vary the look.

Figure 156

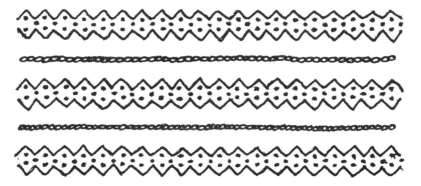

English smocking pattern. Try it in pastels with the flowers in different colors.

Figure 157

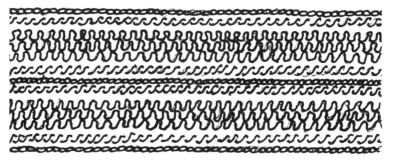

English smocking pattern, good in one color thread.

Figure 158

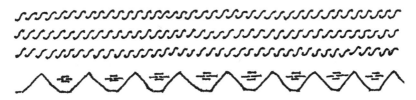

English smocking pattern. A good design for a child's dress, as the trellis stitch at the bottom creates loose gathers.

Instructions for Figure 156

Figure 156 is done starting with the trellis stitch going in opposite directions with flowers spaced evenly between the zigzags. For this project you will need 17 pleated rows. A row of chain stitches separates each of the trellis-stitch designs.

Instructions for Figure 157

Figure 157 starts with a row of chain stitches. For this project you will need 17 pleated rows. Row two is done in the outline stitch, followed by three rows of Van Dyke stitches. These are followed by another row of outline stitches, a row of chain stitches, and another row of outline stitches. Three more rows of Van Dyke stitches, a row of outline stitches, and finally a row of chain stitches will complete the design.

Instructions for Figure 158

Figure 158 illustrates a simple design. For this project you will need 7 pleated rows. It consists of three rows of outline stitches and a row of trellis stitches with a flower worked inside the triangular shapes. This pattern creates a loose gathered effect because of the open trellis stitches at the bottom.

Instructions for Figure 159

Figure 159 starts with a row of Van Dyke stitches and alternates back and forth between that and a zigzag chain-stitched row. For this project you will need 12 pleated rows.

Figure 159

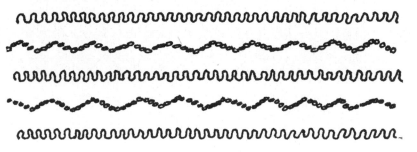

English smocking pattern that gives a tight gather, good for gathering in the fullness at the bottom of a sleeve.

Figure 160

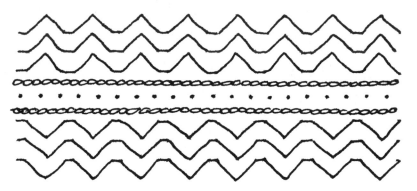

English smocking pattern, nice as the gathering for curtains.

Instructions for Figure 160

For figure 160 you will need 13 pleated rows: three rows of trellis stitches, two rows of chain stitches with flowers in between, and finally three more rows of trellis stitches going the opposite way from before.

Teneriffe apron.

Little girls in Smocked outfits with their Easter baskets.

Close-up details of Smocking for a pinafore.

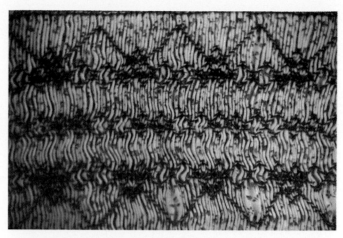

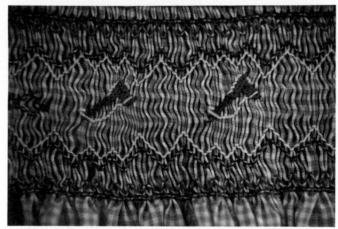

Smocked stick horses.

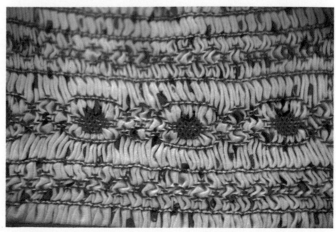

Some Smocked apples.

7

TATTING

My fascination with the vanishing needlework arts started with this particular technique. I attended an old-fashioned quilting bee one afternoon years ago, and noticed a woman sitting in a big easy chair off in the corner. She was working with some pearl cotton and a little oval tool I had never seen before. When I asked the obvious questions, she replied, without ever slowing the in and out motion of her hands, that she was tatting, and that "thing" was called a shuttle. Taking a closer took at the work she had completed, I asked if she would be willing to teach me and where I could obtain supplies. She immediately pulled another shuttle and a ball of thread from her workbasket, and said, "How would right now be?" Believe it or not, it only took her a few minutes to teach me the basics. I would have liked to photograph her and some of her work for this chapter, but she was not available.

Since that time, however, I have met Helen Hansen, another tatting expert. She has expanded my knowledge of the art, and permitted me to photograph some of her beautiful projects, many of which are original patterns.

Tatting consists of only one knot, called a double stitch, and a few picots, which are worked in groups over a single thread and then drawn together to form rings and chains. Many sizes of thread may be used to create different effects, and you will become very fast after a little practice with the shuttle.

Some Tatted edgings for handkerchiefs.

Figure 161 *Details from the tatted doily pictured on page 148, made by Mrs. Helen Hansen. It measures a full yard across!*

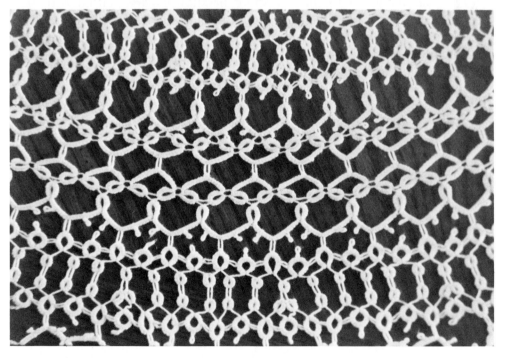

Figure 162

Mrs. Helen Hansen shows some of her handkerchiefs edged with tatting.

Figure 163

Details of handkerchief edgings.

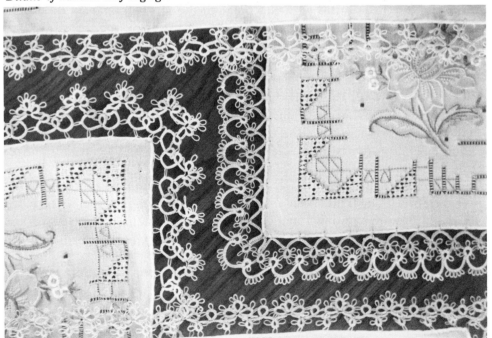

Tatting originated in Europe and was popular during the latter part of the eighteenth century. The French called it *frivolité*, the Italians *occhi*, and in oriental countries the old name is *makouk*. The English called it tatting, and immigrants from many countries brought the art with them to America.

Handkerchiefs, pillowcases, sheets, dresser scarves, and table linens may all be trimmed with a tatted edge, but my favorite way to use it is on clothing. When you become confident in making the knots you might even want to attempt a doily or a complete tablecloth or bedspread.

Supplies Needed

* Tatting shuttle
* One ball Knit-Cro-Sheen
* Regular sewing thread for finishing

Construction

Insert the thread through the little hole in the shuttle bobbin and tie a knot. Holding the shuttle with the point to the left side and on top, wind the thread in a counter-clockwise direction. Do not wind the thread beyond the edges of the shuttle or too tightly.

Unwind 15 to 18 inches of thread from the shuttle and hold it between the thumb and index finger of the left hand about 2 inches from the end. Now wrap it up over the extended middle finger and the slightly bent ring and little fingers. Grasp it again between the thumb and index finger. See figures 164 and 165.

You have now formed a circle around the left hand, and the middle finger must be extended to tighten the slack.

Holding the shuttle with your index finger and thumb of the right hand, pull the thread out tight. Now twist your right hand so the palm is toward you, then forward and down in a circular motion to wrap the thread over the fingers as shown in figures 166 and 167.

Insert the shuttle through the circle thread between the index and middle fingers of the left hand. Now pull it back over the top of the circle thread

Figure 164

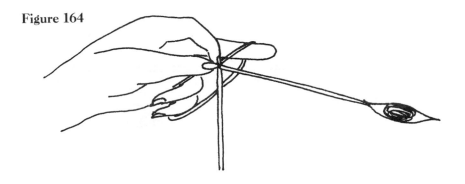

Hook thread with ring and little fingers of left hand. Wrap it over middle finger and grasp between thumb and index fingers.

Figure 165

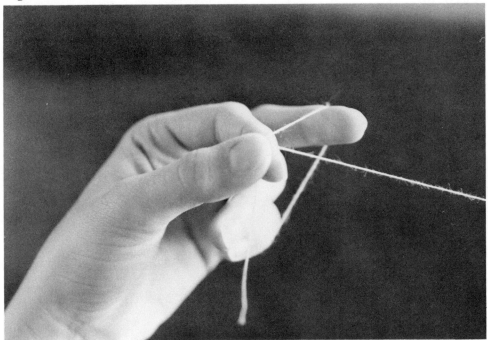

Figure 166

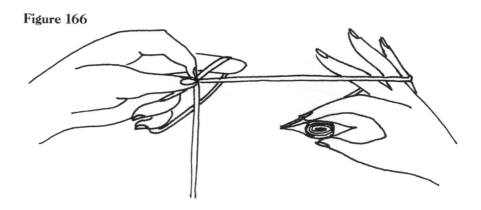

Hold shuttle with right hand. Circle right hand toward you, forward and down, wrapping thread over fingers.

Figure 167

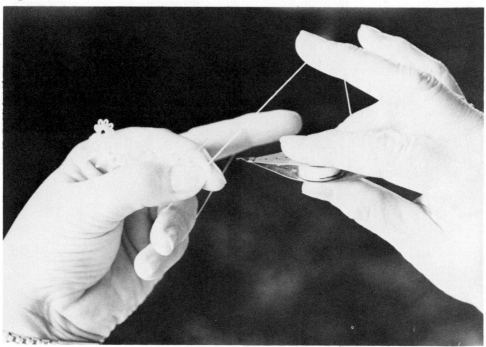

Figure 168

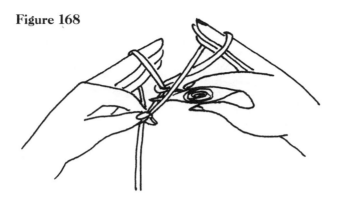

Insert shuttle through the circle thread between the index and middle fingers of left hand. Pull it back over the top of the circle thread, then under the shuttle thread that is on the fingers of the tatting hand.

Figure 169

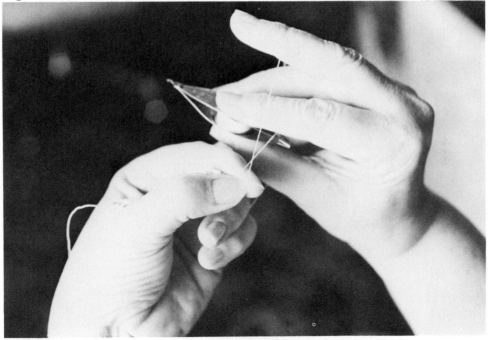

Figure 170

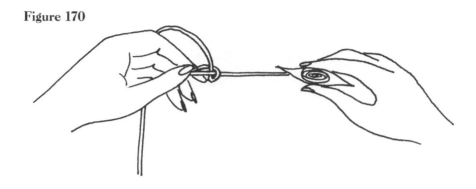

Drop middle finger of left hand to let thread loose. Pull shuttle thread tight.

Figure 171

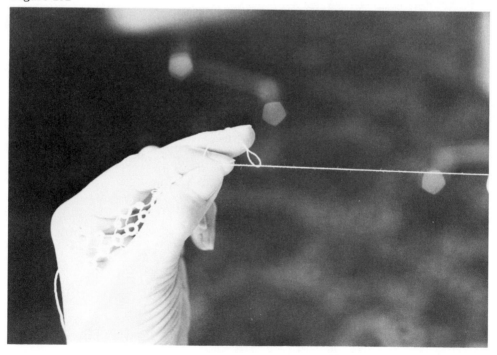

and under the shuttle thread that was over the fingers of the right hand. See figures 168 and 169.

To tighten the thread, drop the middle finger of the left hand letting the circle thread loose, then pull on the shuttle thread until it is tight. See figures 170 and 171.

Now tighten the circle thread again by extending the middle finger with a small jerking motion. See figures 172 and 173.

This completes the first half of the double stitch. To do the second half, bring the shuttle toward the left hand passing over the circle thread and then coming through the circle backward in the same spot as before. See figures 174 and 175.

Again, drop the middle finger of the left hand to slacken the circle thread. Pull the shuttle thread tight, then tighten the circle thread by extending the middle finger with a jerk. This completes the second half of the double stitch. See figures 176 and 177.

It is important at this point that you check to see whether this double stitch will slip back and forth along the circle thread.

Make another double stitch so you have two right together.

To make the first picot (the little loop of thread that stands out beyond the double stitches), make the first half of the double stitch as usual, but don't tighten the circle thread with the jerking motion. Instead, leave about $1/4$ inch slack as shown in figures 178 and 179.

Complete the second half of the knot as usual. Your work should now look like figures 180 and 181.

Make two more double stitches, then form another picot. See figure 182.

Repeat the step above. See figure 183.

Now make two more double stitches. See figure 184.

At this point, you will drop the circle thread from the left hand and, pulling on the shuttle thread, slide all the double stitches together until they form a ring. See figure 185.

Grasp the thread with the left hand again about $1/4$ inch from the ring, form the circle around your fingers and you are ready to start making double stitches again. After you have made two double stitches, you will have to join the ring you are making now to the previous ring through the picot. To do this, lay the picot over the circle thread at the point where it goes over the index finger. See figures 186 and 187.

Using the hook on the shuttle, pull the circle thread through the picot. See figures 188 and 189.

Pull it far enough so you can slip the whole shuttle through the loop.

Figure 172

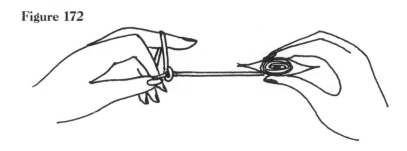

Tighten circle thread by extending middle finger with a jerking motion. This completes first half of the double stitch.

Figure 173

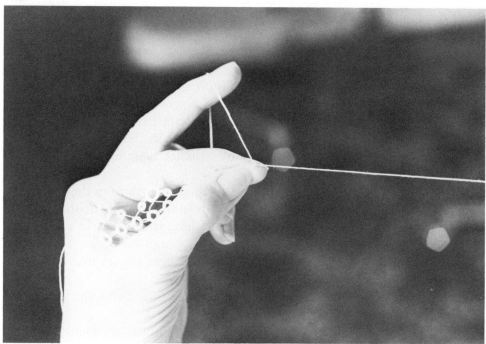

Figure 174

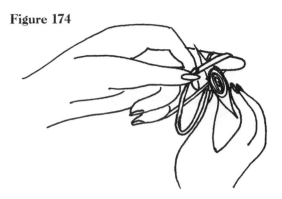

*To begin second half of double stitch, bring the shuttle over
the circle thread, then back through the circle.*

Figure 175

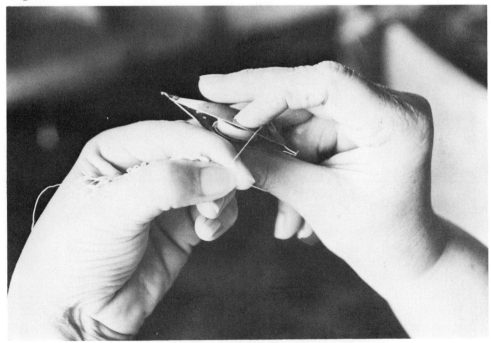

Figure 176

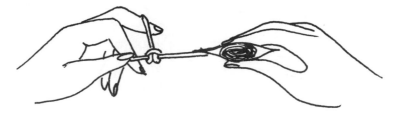

Drop middle finger of left hand to slacken circle thread. Pull shuttle thread tight. Extend middle finger with a jerk to tighten circle thread.

Figure 177

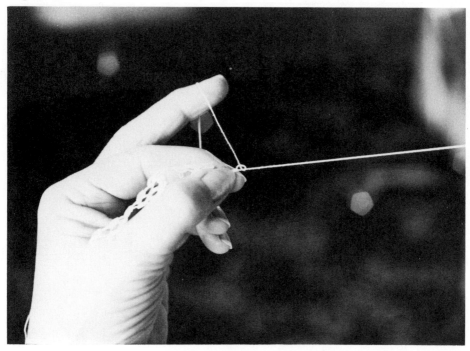

Figure 178

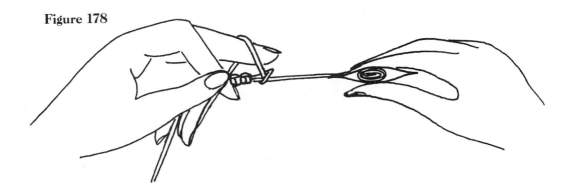

Picot construction: Allow ¹/₄ inch slack after completing the first half of a double stitch. Finish second half of the stitch as before.

Figure 179

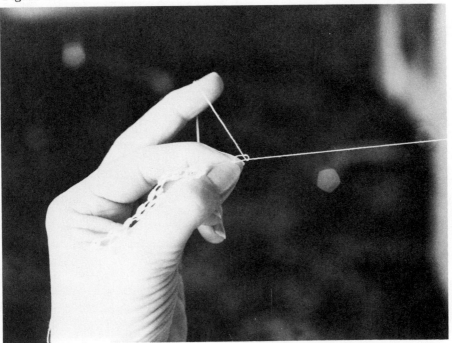

Figure 180

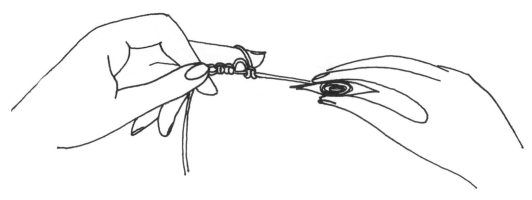

Completed knot—double stitch separated by picot.

Figure 181

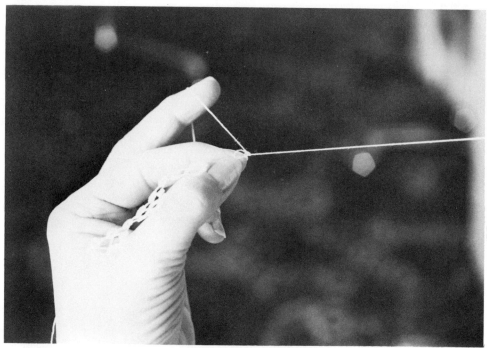

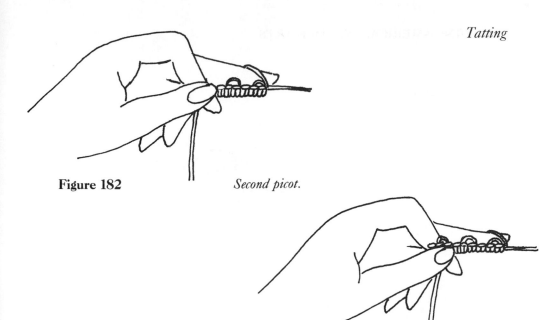

Figure 182   *Second picot.*

Figure 183   *Third picot.*

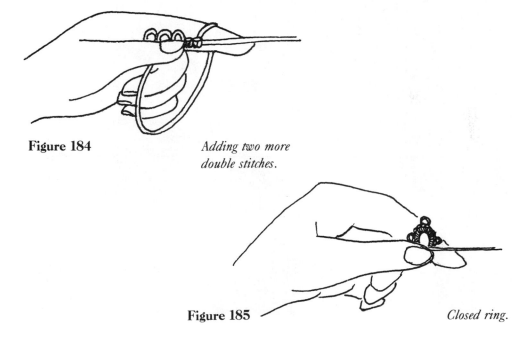

Figure 184   *Adding two more
double stitches.*

Figure 185   *Closed ring.*

Figure 186

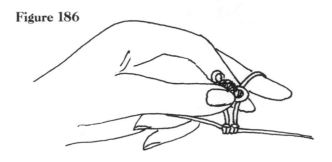

Connecting picots, step 1: Lay picot over circle thread at the point where it goes over index finger.

Figure 187

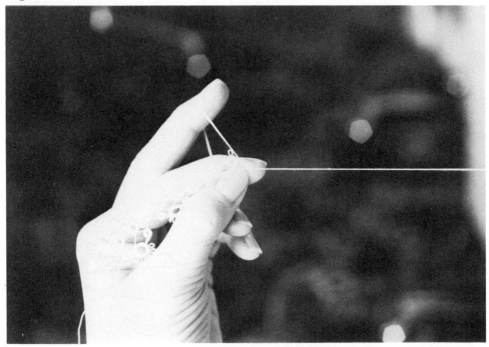

Figure 188

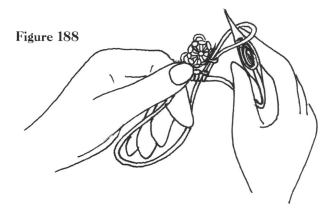

Connecting picots, step 2: With the hook of the shuttle, pull circle thread through the picot.

Figure 189

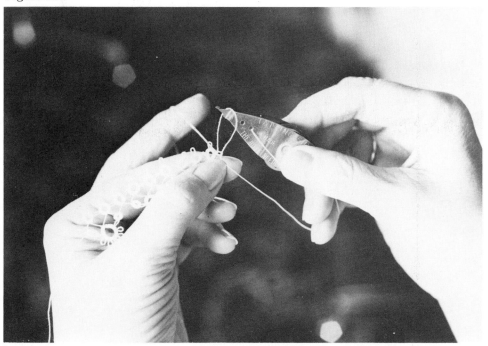

Figure 190

Two rings.

Tighten the shuttle thread and then the circle thread. Complete the stitch by making the second half of a double stitch.

Make two double stitches. Form a picot. Make two more double stitches and form another picot. Make two last double stitches. Drop the circle thread again and tighten your second ring. See figure 190.

Continue forming rings and joining them at the picots.

Finishing Techniques

Lay the tatting face down on your ironing board and anchor each top picot with a pin as shown in figure 191.

Spray lightly with spray starch, and without removing pins, cover with a damp press cloth, and press with a medium hot (cotton) iron being careful not to slide the iron.

Remove the press cloth and allow the tatting to air dry completely before moving.

To attach, use a whip stitch and regular sewing thread.

Figure 191  *Blocking.*

Suggested Uses

* Edging for children's clothing as shown in figure 192

* Edging for a handkerchief as shown in figure 163

* Edging for a tablecloth or placemat

* Christmas tree ornament trim

Figure 192

The author's daughter, Skye, in her dress with tatted trim.

Additional Patterns

Instructions for Figure 193

For the large ring—make two double stitches, form a picot; make three more double stitches, form the top picot; make three more double stitches, form a picot; make two more double stitches and close the ring.

For the small ring—make two double stitches; attach to the previous ring through the picot; make three more double stitches, form a picot; make two more double stitches and close the ring.

Continue making large and small rings, joining at the side picots as illustrated in figure 193.

Instructions for Figure 194

The pattern in figure 194 is worked by making rings with multiple picots.

Make two double stitches, then form the side picot; make two more double stitches and then form three picots together, making the center one a little larger than the other two. Make two more double stitches, then form the picot for the other side of the ring. Make two more double stitches and close the ring.

Repeat the above ring until you obtain the desired length of trim.

Instructions for Figure 195

For the small ring—make two double stitches, form the side picot; make two more double stitches, form the top picot; make two more double stitches, form the picot for the other side; make two more double stitches and close the ring.

Make two small rings together and then one large ring.

For the large ring—make two double stitches, attach to the previous ring through the picot; make two more double stitches, form three picots right together; make two more double stitches, form the picot for the other side; make two more double stitches and close the ring. See figure 195.

Instructions for Figure 196

To form the braid pattern shown in diagram 196, you will simply flip the thread over and work the rings in opposite directions.

For the ring—make three double stitches, form a picot; make two double stitches and form another picot; make one double stitch and form a third picot, then make another double stitch and form a fourth picot; make two more double stitches and form the other side picot, then three more double stitches. Close. This is ring A in diagram 196.

Figure 193 *Simple tatted edging pattern with large and small rings.*

Figure 194 *Simple tatted edging pattern with multiple picots.*

Figure 195 *Simple tatted edging pattern with large and small rings and multiple picots.*

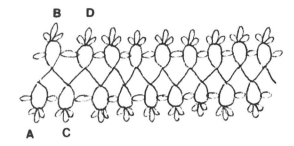

Figure 196 *Tatted braid can be attached to an edge or used as an insert.*

Figure 197 *Tatted braid, a neat edging.*

Flip that picot down and work another ring. This is ring B. Don't attach these two rings.

Flip the work back up, which will put ring A at the top of the work and ring B at the bottom. Construct ring C and attach it to ring A at the side picots as shown.

Flip the work again, make ring D and attach it to ring B.

Continue forming rings, attaching at the sides, and flipping the work after each one.

Instructions for Figure 197

This pattern (figure 197) is worked by flipping the work over in the same manner described in the pattern for figure 196.

For the small rings—make two double stitches and form a picot; make two more double stitches and form another picot; make two more double stitches, form the other side picot; make two more double stitches and close.

For the large rings—make two double stitches and form a picot; make two more double stitches and form three picots in a row; make two more double stitches, form the other side picot; make two more double stitches and close.

133

8

TENERIFFE

The more intricate forms of Teneriffe are worked on a cushion, or on a piece of cardboard much like the Aemelia-ars lace motifs described in Chapter 1. These are beautiful when completed, resembling spider webs. Earlier forms of Teneriffe were known as Brazilian point lace.

To learn this technique, it is easiest to work a simplified version that you can easily do on any fabric that has square markings, such as a gingham check or an evenly woven linen. It is usually a repetition of one pattern done along an edge.

I was given a set of pillowcases with Teneriffe on them for a graduation gift and promptly put them in my cedar chest along with the other needlework items I had collected without labeling where they came from or who had done them. Later, when I found them again, I tried to trace their origin with no luck. I am guessing but cannot verify, as she has passed on, that my grandmother was the one who made them. I did locate a woman who lives near my grandmother's old home who said she taught my grandmother the technique and shared her patterns. This woman has given all her work away through the years, but was willing to share her patterns with me.

Pillowcases and table linens look like you have spent hours on them when they are decorated with Teneriffe, when in reality the weaving technique moves very quickly.

Pillowcases decorated with
Teneriffe in different patterns and colors.

Different types of thread may be used and sometimes it is fun to mix colors within the same pattern.

Supplies Needed

* Embroidery hoops to hold the fabric tight
* Sharp needle size 26
* DMC Pearl Cotton size 8
* $\frac{1}{4}$ yard gingham check fabric ($\frac{1}{4}$ inch size is best for this project)
* Scissors

Construction

Cut a $7\frac{1}{4}$-inch square from the fabric. Find the center point by counting the lines or by folding the piece in half. After marking this point, secure the fabric in the embroidery hoops, centering the marked point. Thread the needle with a long length of thread (32 to 36 inches), and tie a small knot in the end.

Count up $4\frac{1}{2}$ spaces from the center point and over $4\frac{1}{2}$ spaces to the right. Bring your needle *up* from the wrong side of the fabric at this point. Then moving diagonally across the center point to the lower left of the work, take the needle *down* at the corner, nine lines below and nine lines to the left. See figure 199.

Move up one space and bring the needle *up* again. Then moving up seven and to the right nine, take the needle *down* again. See figure 200.

Come *up* one space below. Take the needle *down* five spaces down and nine spaces to the left. See figure 201.

Next move up five spaces and bring the needle *up* again. Take it *down* five spaces below and nine to the right. See figure 202.

Bring it *up* one space below and *down* seven spaces up and nine to the left. See figure 203.

Bring the needle *up* one space above and *down* nine spaces below and nine to the right. See figure 204.

Come *up* one space to the left and *down* seven spaces to the left and nine up. See figure 205.

Come *up* one space to the right and *down* five spaces to the right and nine down. See figure 206.

Come *up* five spaces to the left and *down* five spaces back to the right and nine up. See figure 207.

Figure 199

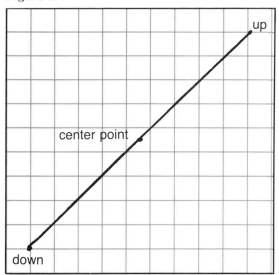

Figure 200

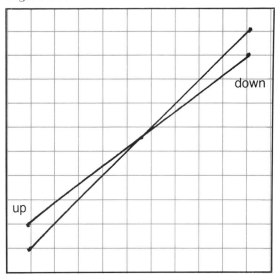

Figure 201

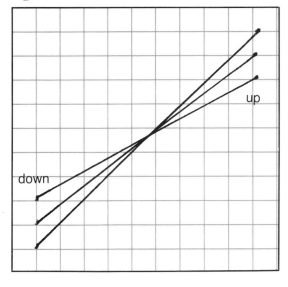

Figure 202

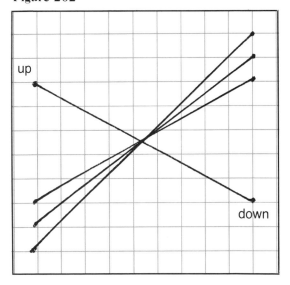

Figure 203

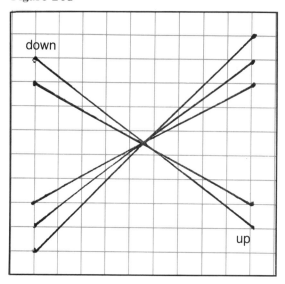

Figure 204

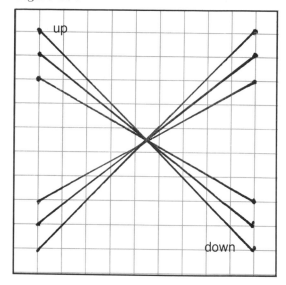

Figure 205

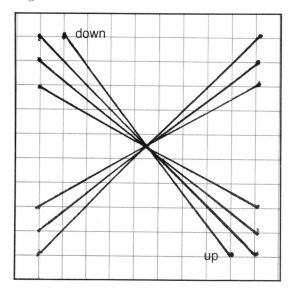

Figure 206

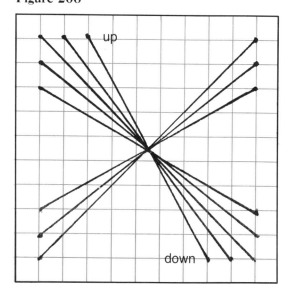

Figure 207

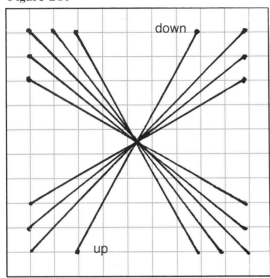

down

up

Figure 208

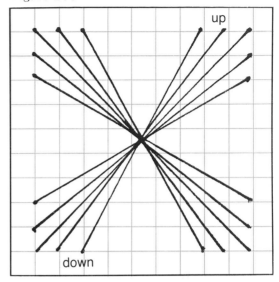

up

down

Figure 209

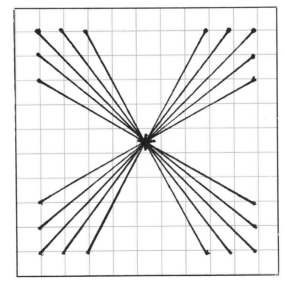

Completed skeleton reinforced at center point.

Figure 210

start

Figure 211

Needle weaving.

Figure 212

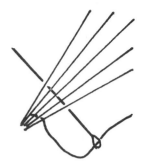

Figure 213

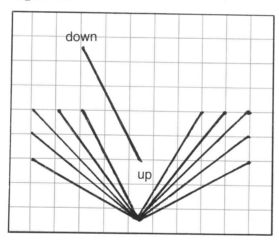

down

up

Figure 214

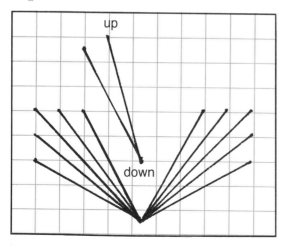

up

down

Figure 215

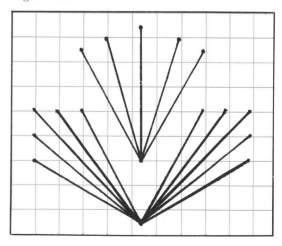

Now come *up* one space to the right and *down* seven spaces to the left and nine down. See figure 208.

Now the skeleton is formed. Bring the needle back up at the approximate center point to reinforce it with a tiny cross. See figure 209. Secure the thread on the wrong side and rethread the needle with a long length of thread.

Bring the needle up at the point shown in diagram 210.

Now weave the needle over and under the five skeleton threads of this leg starting as shown in figure 211. Do not catch the fabric.

Then come back the other way as shown in figure 212.

Repeat this pattern of over, under, over, under, working back and forth and pushing the threads toward the center point. When you reach the end of the shorter skeleton threads, continue wrapping the inside three as far as possible, taking the needle down through the fabric to the back next to the center skeleton thread.

Bring the needle up at the center of the next leg and begin the weaving process again.

When you have finished all four sides, secure the thread on the wrong side.

If you find it necessary to rethread the needle before you have completed all four legs, try to do it between legs so the weaving action won't be interrupted.

To start the outside designs, thread your needle with another long length of thread and tie a knot at the end. Come *up* from the back side $2^1/_2$ spaces above the center point. Go *down* $4^1/_2$ spaces up and $2^1/_2$ spaces to the left. See figure 213.

Come *up* one space to the right and $^1/_2$ space up, and go *down* at the beginning point. See figure 214.

Come *up* $5^1/_2$ spaces above the starting point, and back *down* at the starting point again.

Come *up* $1^1/_2$ spaces to the right and 5 spaces up, and *down* at the starting point.

Come *up* $2^1/_2$ spaces to the right and $4^1/_2$ spaces up, and *down* at the starting point. See figure 215.

Bring the needle up at the starting point to the side of the center skeleton thread again and weave these threads as you did the center legs.

Complete the outside design on the other three sides.

Finishing Techniques

Lay your piece face down on a thick towel and press from the wrong side.

Figure 216

Figure 217

Hot pad decorated in the Teneriffe pattern described in this chapter.

Apron decorated with teneriffe and cross stitch. Details are shown in figure 226, and the actual pattern is shown in figure 227.

Suggested Uses

* Hot pads (see figure 216)

* Trim the border of an apron (see figure 217)

* Trim the border of a pillowcase (see figure 198)

To trim a border, repeat a design over and over along the edge, or alternate two designs back and forth.

Additional Patterns

Instructions for Figures 218 and 219

Lay the base threads as shown in figure 219, and then weave the thread back and forth to achieve the finished look pictured in figure 218.

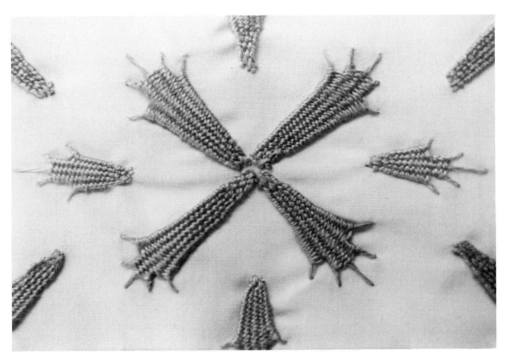

Figure 218

Figure 219

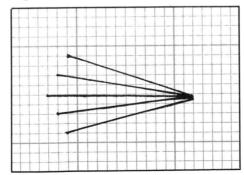

Instructions for Figures 220 and 221

The base threads are laid here exactly like they were in the first pattern described in this chapter. The difference is that there are seven legs per corner instead of five. For the base thread layout see figure 221, and for the finished effect see figure 220.

Figure 220

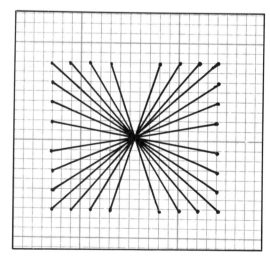

Figure 221

144

Instructions for Figures 222 and 223

To lay the base threads for the pattern shown in figure 222, follow the lines given in figure 223. The threads are then woven over and under from side to side crossing the center point, as before on other patterns.

Figure 222

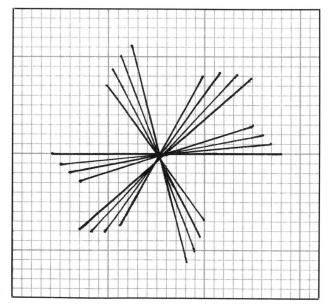

Figure 223

Figure 224

Figure 225

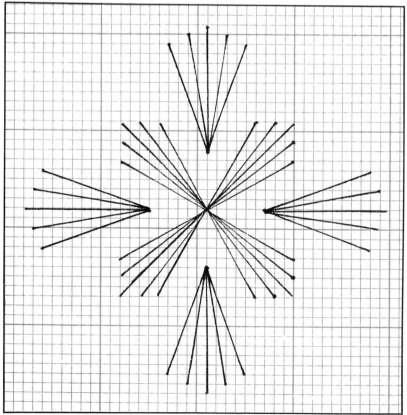

Instructions for Figures 224 and 225

The pattern shown in figures 224 and 225 is done exactly like the one described at the beginning of this chapter, except that the base threads are laid closer together. This makes the design appear longer at each corner.

Instructions for Figures 226 and 227

The pattern for the Teneriffe part of this design is a familiar one to you by now, but this time some cross stitch designs have been added. Size 5 Pearl Cotton was used here instead of size 8.

Figure 226

Figure 227

Close-up details of apron shown in figure 217.

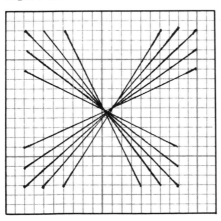

GLOSSARY

Aemilia-ars Lace A needle-made lace constructed of thread on skeleton base threads in small squares called motifs.

Bar Tacks Used to hold the skeleton threads to the cardboard during construction of Aemilia-ars lace.

Bars Covered base threads used to secure the cut-away portions of fabric in cutwork and Hardanger.

Base Threads Usually three threads that are covered with buttonhole stitches, or corded in needle-made laces.

Block A finishing method used to help laces hold their proper shape.

Brides Another name for the bars used in cutwork.

Buttonhole Stitch An embroidery stitch used in Aemilia-ars lace and cutwork. Shown in figures 4 and 33.

Chain Stitch A surface embroidery stitch. Illustrated in figure 145.

Cord To wrap the needle thread around base threads.

Cutwork Lacelike designs worked on firmly woven linen mostly in buttonhole stitches with portions cut away to achieve an open look.

DMC Pearl Cotton A twisted thread used in sizes 5 or 8 when working many needle-work projects.

Netted doily.

Doily A small mat used as a decoration or to protect a surface.

Double Stitch The stitch used in tatting. Shown in figures 164–177.

Frivolité The French name for tatting.

Hardanger Norwegian embroidery worked in kloster blocks to form geometric designs with woven bars, filling stitches, and cut-away portions.

Hedebo Danish needlepoint lace used to trim edges or as inserts.

Hedebo Buttonhole Stitch Different from the buttonhole stitch used in Aemilia-ars lace and cutwork. Shown in figures 84 and 85.

Hemstitch An ornamental stitch, made by pulling out several parallel threads and tying the cross threads into small bunches.

Italian Cutwork The most difficult form of cutwork, done in squares with cut and pulled threads and a lot of surface embroidery.

Kloster Block A group of satin stitches of an uneven number, worked over an even number of fabric threads in Hardanger.

Knit-Cro-Sheen A heavier weight thread than DMC Pearl Cotton.

Lattice Base Another name used for the skeleton threads that Aemilia-ars lace is constructed around.

Makouk The ancient oriental name for tatting.

Mesh Stick In netting, the stick around which knots are constructed.

Motifs Squares of lace.

Netting An ancient knotting technique worked over a mesh stick.

Netting Needle An instrument with two small prongs at each end. Used to hold the thread and weave it through the wrapping in netting.

Occhi The Italian name for tatting.

Outline Stitch An embroidery stitch used for surface designs. Shown in figure 138.

Picot A small loop of thread that extends outward from the base. Three different methods are shown in figures 46 through 52.

Renaissance Cutwork The main feature of this type of cutwork is the bars.

Richelieu Cutwork A form of cutwork where picots are worked on the bars as decorations.

Running Stitch Used in cutwork, and shown in figure 33.

Satin Stitch An embroidery stitch used in groups to create a solid effect. The stitches run parallel to each other and are as close as possible.

Selvage A specially woven edge that prevents cloth from raveling.

Simple Cutwork Cutwork that has no bars or picots. The open or cut-away portions are supported by the design itself.

Size 100 Thread A very fine and lightweight thread.

Skeleton Threads The base threads that are laid first and then covered to form an Aemilia-ars lace motif.

Smocking Three different methods of holding gathers in an ornamental way.

Speed-Cro-Sheen Thread, heavier than DMC Pearl Cotton.

Straight of Grain Vertical and horizontal threads running exactly perpendicular to each other throughout a piece of fabric.

Tatting Groups of double stitches made with a shuttle, forming rings and chains.

Tatting Shuttle A small oval device used to hold the thread in tatting.

Teneriffe Weaving the base threads of the designs in this form of needlework creates a weblike effect.

Trellis Stitch Used in smocking and shown in figures 139 and 140.

Trousseau A bride's clothes and linens.

Van Dyke Stitch Used in smocking and shown in figures 145 through 148.

Venetian Needlepoint A type of lace that some forms of cutwork stem from.

Warp Lengthwise threads in a piece of fabric.

Weft Crosswise threads in a piece of fabric.

Wrapped Bars Used in cutwork and Hardanger. Shown in figure 45.

Supplies used for various projects, including netting needles and tatting shuttle.

SUPPLIES

The following is a list of wholesale outlets you may write to for information about retail stores in your area that carry these supplies.

Fabrics

ZeAnn's Needlework Supplies
3692 South 4225 West
West Valley City, UT 84120

Sabra Supply Co.
P. O. Box 35575
Houston, TX 77035

Notions

Lacis
2990 Adeline Street
Berkeley, CA 94703

Smocking Supplies

Little Miss Muffet
316 Nancy Lynn Lane
P. O. Box 10912
Knoxville, TN 37919

Threads

DMC
107 Trumbull Street
Elizabeth, NJ 07206

If you wish to order any of the items listed in this book by mail, you can write to ZeAnn's at the above address to request prices and shipping information.

Title page of old needlework book, copyright 1887.

DEDICATED TO H.R.H. PRINCESS LOUISE, MARCHIONESS OF LORNE.

THE

DICTIONARY OF NEEDLEWORK,

AN

ENCYCLOPÆDIA OF ARTISTIC, PLAIN, AND FANCY NEEDLEWORK,

DEALING FULLY WITH THE DETAILS OF ALL THE STITCHES EMPLOYED, THE METHOD OF WORKING,
THE MATERIALS USED, THE MEANING OF TECHNICAL TERMS, AND, WHERE NECESSARY,
TRACING THE ORIGIN AND HISTORY OF THE VARIOUS WORKS DESCRIBED.

ILLUSTRATED WITH UPWARDS OF 800 WOOD ENGRAVINGS,
AND
COLOURED PLATES.

PLAIN SEWING, TEXTILES, DRESSMAKING, APPLIANCES, AND TERMS,

By S. F. A. CAULFEILD,

Author of "Sick Nursing at Home," "Desmond," "Avenele," and Papers on Needlework in "The Queen," "Girl's Own Paper,"
"Cassell's Domestic Dictionary," &c.

CHURCH EMBROIDERY, LACE, AND ORNAMENTAL NEEDLEWORK,

By BLANCHE C. SAWARD,

Author of "Church Festival Decorations," and Papers on Fancy and Art Work in "The Bazaar," "Artistic Amusements,"
"Girl's Own Paper," &c.

SECOND EDITION.

LONDON:
L. UPCOTT GILL, 170, STRAND, W.C.

1887.

BIBLIOGRAPHY

Caulfeild, S.F.A. DICTIONARY OF NEEDLEWORK. London: L. Upcott Gill, 1887.

Durand, Dianne. DIANNE DURAND'S SMOCKING STITCHES. Little Miss Muffet, Inc., 1980.

"Good Housekeeping Gingham Embroidery." Hearst Corporation, 1963. (GHN 750)

LEARN TO TAT. Coats & Clark, 1974. (Book No. 240)

Nelson, Vera C. NELSON BOOK OF NETTING. Salt Lake City: Frank J. Nelson, Jr., 1949.

"Old Time Needlework." Feb-Mar 1977 and Nov 1977.

Ryan, Mildred Graves. THE COMPLETE ENCYCLOPEDIA OF STITCHERY. New York: Doubleday & Co., Inc., 1979.

Thomas, Mary. MARY THOMAS'S EMBROIDERY BOOK. London & Southampton: Camelot Press Ltd., 1936.

My mother and I working on illustrations.

INDEX